Cognition
and Curriculum

THE JOHN DEWEY LECTURE—NUMBER EIGHTEEN

The John Dewey Lecture is delivered annually under the sponsership of the John Dewey Society. This book is an elaboration of the Lecture given in 1979. The intention of the series is to provide a setting where able thinkers from various sectors of our intellectual life can direct their most searching thought to problems that involve the relation of education to culture. Arrangements for the presentation and publication of the Lecture are under the direction of the John Dewey Society Commission on Lectures.

Gerald M. Reagan, *Chairperson and Editor*
The Ohio State University

Cognition and Curriculum

A Basis for Deciding What to Teach

Elliot W. Eisner

New York & London

Cognition and Curriculum

Longman Inc., 19 West 44th Street, New York, N.Y. 10036
Associated companies, branches, and representatives
throughout the world.

Developmental Editor: Nicole Benevento
Editorial and Design Supervisor: Diane Perlmuth
Cover Design: Dan Serrano
Manufacturing and Production Supervisor: Robin B. Besofsky

Library of Congress Cataloging in Publication Data

Eisner, Elliot W.
   Cognition and curriculum.

   (The John Dewey Society lecture series; no. 18, 1981)
   Bibliography: p.
   Includes index.
   1. Basic education—United States. 2. Education—United States—
Evaluation. I. Title. II. Series.
LC1035.6.E36   370'.973   81-11804
ISBN 0-582-28149-0   AACR2

Manufactured in the United States of America
9 8 7 6 5 4 3

I believe that the individual who is to be educated is
a social individual, and that society is an organic
union of individuals. If we eliminate the social factor
from the child we are left only with an abstraction;
if we eliminate the individual factor from society, we
are left only with an inert and lifeless mass. Education, therefore, must begin with a psychological insight
into the child's capacities, interests, and habits. It
must be controlled at every point by reference to these
same considerations. These powers, interests, and
habits must be continually interpreted—we must know
what they mean. They must be translated into terms of
their social equivalents—into terms of what they are
capable of in the way of social service.

John Dewey
My Pedagogic Creed, 1897

Contents

Foreword

In *Art as Experience* John Dewey wrote:

> The difference between the esthetic and the intellectual is thus one of the place where emphasis falls in the constant rhythm that marks the interaction of the live creature with his surroundings.

Elliot Eisner extends the work of Dewey and applies the underlying ideas to curriculum and evaluation in contemporary American education. He is systematically critical of the current "back to basics" movement and is particularly vehement in opposing the diminution and even elimination of the arts. In a clear, brief, yet thorough analysis, he explains the role of the senses in concept formation, the way different modes of expression make different demands on intelligence and thus contribute to our efforts to extract meaning from experience. Such analysis is necessary if we are to escape the ever-narrowing conceptions of what schools ought to do and how we should evaluate the results of schooling.

In 1938, in *Experience and Education*, Dewey criticized the widespread confusion concerning the appropriate meaning of "progressive" education. The need is every bit as serious today to examine the movement toward a narrow conception of the curriculum sloganized as "basics." This movement is supported by the limited conception that intelligence only includes verbal and mathematical reasoning and that the arts are based on emotions and embodied in those who are talented. Such a limited notion of intelligence is strongly supported by an unduly restricted conception of science and the methods of science, upon which currently dominant methods of evaluation are based. There is an interlocking and mutually reinforcing set of relationships between college entrance requirements, techniques of evaluation, standardized testing, narrowing of the curriculum, and the educational frustration and failure of large segments of the population. Ultimately, this interlocking set of events will be broken only by a more generous conception of human intelligence, a conception supported by excellent evidence from various fields of inquiry.

It is to be hoped that Elliot Eisner's work will shake up educational decision makers as Dewey's *Experience And Education* did. It is time that both curriculum and evaluation reflect the many faces of intelligence and that professional educators cease merely responding to the public's desire for "older, simpler and more predictable ways." Eisner's work reflects Dewey's earlier recognition that: "Thinking directly in terms of colors, tones, images, is a different operation technically from thinking in words. But only superstition will hold that, because the meaning of paintings and symphonies cannot be translated into words, or that of poetry into prose, therefore thought is monopolized by the latter. If all meanings could be adequately expressed by words, the arts of painting and music would not exist." Professor Eisner has opened a serious dialogue concerning the appropriate breadth of a balanced curriculum and the forging of new methods for evaluating the rich and varied expressions of human intelligence.

Louis Fischer
University of Massachusetts, Amherst
May 1981

Preface

Among the major developments in American education during the past decade, two have assumed particular importance. The first is the result of growing public concern that the quality of American schools is declining; the second stems from efforts to develop new and more effective methods of educational evaluation. Concern for the quality of education is most often expressed as the desire to return to what is truly fundamental in schooling, that is, acquiring literacy and achieving competency in the use of numbers. In sloganese, the demand has been to "return to the basics."

As for evaluation, the desire has been, on the one hand, to develop methods that could be used to determine whether basic skills—so-called minimum competencies—are being attained and, on the other hand, to go beyond conventional methods of evaluation in order to provide more useful information both to the public at large and to those who work in the schools.

The consequences of the "back to the basics" movement and the desire to develop better ways to evaluate are two of several themes that run throughout this small book in which I have attempted to point out some of the effects of what is termed the "basic skills" approach in education. Some of the central issues and some of the concerns of educators and the public are identified in Chapter 1, and some of the practical effects of these concerns on teaching, on curriculum, and on the students the schools are intended to serve are discussed as well.

This identification of issues and concerns only serves, however, to introduce the major topics that this book addresses: the identification of the role of the senses in human conceptualization and the description of the forms humans use to make their conceptualizations public. The phrase "forms of representation" is used to characterize the latter.

The thesis that I have developed argues that the senses play a fundamental role in concept formation and that because the senses are qualitatively specific—that is, each is biologically designed to pick up some, but not all kinds of information from the environment—the kinds of concepts that humans form relate directly to the kind of content that each of the senses makes possible. I argue, further, that, because concept formation is dependent upon sensory material, the kind of meaning that one can convey is profoundly influenced by the sensory qualities emphasized by particular forms of representation. The meanings secured in auditory forms of representation—music, for example—are not *literally* translatable to other forms. Thus, insofar as education is concerned with developing the individual's ability to secure diverse forms of meaning through experience, then the ability to encode and decode the content embodied in different forms of representation is also of crucial importance. Such ability can be regarded as a form of literacy. The concept of literacy, as I have used it, is not limited to things said; it extends to things represented. I choose to use the term generically as the power to encode or decode meaning through any of the forms that humans use to represent what they have come to know. The argument for this view of cognition, which appears in Chapters 2 and 3, provides the basic thesis for this book.

It is in Chapter 4 that I deal with the implications of this view for questions related to curriculum content and to educational evaluation. If meaning is specific to the forms of representation used and if the schools are or should be concerned with expanding the student's ability to construe meaning from experience, then determining which forms should receive attention within the school curriculum constitutes one of the most fundamental of educational decisions. Furthermore, if evaluators are interested in conveying the range and diversity of meanings construed in their study of educational settings, then the ability to use a variety of forms competently is necessary. A restrictive use of forms of representation imposes severe constraints on what can be conveyed. Thus, the ideas developed in Chapters 2 and 3 have significant implications for both what we teach and how we evaluate.

In developing the thesis presented in this book, I am aware that others, particularly philosophers such as David Hume, for example, have traversed these paths before. More specifically, I owe a great intellectual debt to Rudolf Arnheim, to Suzanne Langer, and, of course, to John Dewey. Their work has had an extraordinary effect on my thinking. If I have a contribution to make, it is not so much in the formulation of the basic concepts—although I hope that at least some of them are fresh

—but in the application of the ideas to educational theory and practice. I hope that what I say will ultimately help to broaden our view of both curriculum and evaluation, two fields that in my opinion are in need of some new models of practice. The curriculum of schools in the United States is constrained by the public's anxiety over falling test scores. Evaluation practices in schools are constrained by the public's demand that payoff be measured, thus requiring the use of a form of representation that has its own restrictions. In neither area do the practices look far enough into the possibilities of the human mind. Traditional expectations loom too large. If this small book makes some contribution to a wider view of curriculum and evaluation, I shall be satisfied.

I wish to express my gratitude to a number of organizations that have made it possible for me to prepare this work. The John Dewey Society asked me to deliver the John Dewey Lecture in Chicago in 1979 and to prepare this book in connection with that lecture. The Spencer Foundation with its typical graciousness provided financial support to assist in the preparation of the manuscript. To its President, H. Thomas James, I express my deep gratitude. The Northwest Regional Educational Laboratory also provided support and encouragement, particularly with respect to that portion of the book that focuses upon evaluation. I am very grateful to each of these institutions for their help.

I want to express my appreciation to Irving Segal of the Educational Testing Service and to Nancy Stein of the University of Chicago for their constructive critique of the manuscript. Their advice was useful and much appreciated. Dick Snow of the School of Education at Stanford University and Gabby Solomon of the Hebrew University in Jerusalem worked with me during the initial conceptualizations and provided encouragement and assistance from their perspective in psychology. I offer them my thanks.

I also want to express my thanks to my secretary at Stanford University, Mrs. Constance Barrell, for her good humor and competence in helping me deal with the seemingly countless demands that would otherwise seriously have impeded my writing. Finally, I want to thank my wife, Ellie, for not only typing the manuscript but for providing the kinds of candid reactions and marginal notes that alerted me to sections needing further clarification and elaboration. Her comments almost always hit the mark.

Elliot W. Eisner
Stanford University
February 1981

1

What Is Basic in Education?

If one believes what one reads in the newspapers, American education is in a state of significant decline. Not only do the newspapers tell the story, but magazines, books, and television also lament the decline of educational quality. Consider the following lead paragraph from an article in *Time*:

> Like some vast jury reluctantly arriving at a verdict, politicians, educators and especially millions of parents have come to believe that the U.S. public schools are in serious trouble. Violence keeps making headlines. Test scores keep dropping. Debate rages over whether or not one-fifth or more adult Americans are functionally illiterate. High school graduates go so far as to sue their school systems because they got respectable grades and a diploma but cannot fill in job application forms correctly. Experts confirm that students today get at least 25% more As and Bs than they did 15 years ago, but know less. A government-funded nationwide survey group, the National Assessment of Educational Progress, reports that in science, writing, social studies and mathematics the achievement of U.S. 17-year-olds has dropped regularly over the past decade.[1]

Or, if more scholarly prose suits, then consider the following:

> Through the nineteen forties, fifties and up to the mid-sixties, achievement test scores steadily increased. Since then, many test scores dropped. The reported test score declines are more dramatic in recent years

and most evident for higher grades. They are especially pronounced in verbal tests, but hold for nearly all tested areas.[2]

Whether one's information comes from polemically written magazine articles or from the pages of more reflective journals, the story is largely the same. Test scores have been falling since 1963 and signal the decline of our schools. One of the early indexes of this decline was the pattern of scores that was recorded on the Scholastic Aptitude Test. From 1963 to 1977 there has been a drop of forty-nine points in verbal scores and of thirty-one points in mathematical scores.[3] Since this was thought to be an early indicator of a drop in the quality of schooling, it stimulated the examination of other indicators of academic achievement to determine whether there had been a corresponding decline. There was. Declines have occurred in the American College Testing Program, in the Minnesota Scholastic Aptitude Test, in the tests used by the National Assessment of Educational Progress, and in the Comprehensive Tests of Basic Skills.[4]

Concern for decline in achievement was also being expressed by university faculties. There seemed to be virtual unanimity among university professors that students could not read as well as they once could and that their ability to write a clear English paragraph was small. To cope with the problem, remedial programs were initiated in colleges and universities throughout the country to teach what faculty members believed should have been learned in the elementary and secondary schools.[5] Such programs were not limited to state universities or to city or community colleges. Prestigious and highly selective universities such as Stanford and Harvard also felt obliged to improve the reading and writing skills of their students. Even, it seems, some secondary school students in the upper 2 to 3 percent academically of all students at their age level were believed to be in serious need of remediation. And if these students were in trouble, one can just imagine the state of the rest.

University professors had customarily complained about the quality of secondary schools and the abilities of secondary school students, but this time their complaints were supported by data based on the results of standardized achievement tests administered through national and state testing programs. For one reason or another—and the reasons are far from clear—the ability of students to read, to write, and to compute was not as good as it once was, and surely it was not as good as it ought to be. The solution seemed perfectly simple. By going "back to the basics" at both the elementary and secondary levels of schooling, a situation that had never been good in the first place and had become even worse in recent years could be remedied.

"Back to the basics," like many effective slogans, gained popular support. How could one argue with emphasizing what is basic? And in a period when art nouveau, the 1920s, and the romantic nostalgia of pre-World War II America were enjoying a rebirth, going backward rather than forward seemed preferable. The past almost always has a rosy glow.

As for "the basics" there seemed to be little ambiguity about what was involved—at least for those who have not thought deeply about education. What was basic in education was being able to read, to write, and to compute. Virtually everyone believed that these skills had been neglected if not abandoned altogether during the 1960s and the 1970s, that seductive period in which educational innovation, the new math, Title III of the Elementary and Secondary Education Act, and the belief that students should participate in deciding what they should study were frequently discussed. After all, the evidence of educational "innovation" was physically present: architecturally open schools, computer terminals in classrooms, extensive varieties of curricular kits for teaching the educationally exotic. And the nonphysical aspects of educational policy also seemed to contribute significantly to educational decline: flexible scheduling, nongraded schools, social promotion, team teaching, multiage grouping. Whether these practices were widely used in the nation's schools or whether architecturally open schools were also educationally open were questions that were seldom raised. Simply the *idea* of their use was enough to provide a center around which a concerned public could rally. What percentage of elementary and secondary schools were built on an open plan? And of those so built, how many expressed in their educational practice the view of teaching or learning expressed in their architecture? How many elementary schools departed significantly from a heavy emphasis on the three Rs? In how many secondary schools were course requirements in English and mathematics reduced or withdrawn? For many dismayed elementary school principals and teachers, there is no way to go back to the basics because they do not know how to go back to what they never left in the first place.

Within the Cultural Climate

The nuances of such complexities do not lend themselves well to treatment in the mass media. When Walter Cronkite broadcasts a program on prime time television to 50 million people addressing the question, "Is Anyone Out There Learning?" the question becomes a rhetorical device designed to capture interest and to accuse by innuendo. The public schools as a whole, like the United States Congress as a whole, are unaccustomed to accolades. To appraise the schools and not to find them wanting is, it seems, a tacit admission that one lacks standards. It is far easier, at least as far as these institutions are concerned, to criticize rather than to praise.

In my opinion, however, the criticism that has been leveled against the schools is part of a more general climate in the United States. The feelings that people seem to have about the quality of schooling are not isolated from other tendencies in the culture at large. Consider capital punishment. In 1977 the Supreme Court ruled in a landmark decision, *Furman* v. *Georgia*, that the death penalty was "cruel and unusual punishment" because it did not conform to minimum standards of retributive justice.[6] The court held that the administration of the death penalty has been "rare, arbitrary and discriminatory." The vast majority of those on death row were either black or belonged to other minority groups. Of rape offenders, for example, nonwhites have been executed at a rate six times that of whites.[7] Thirty-seven states rescinded these discriminatory statutes only to reinstitute them with more stringently defined criteria.[8] The opportunity to treat capital offenders in noncapital ways was rejected. While only one country in Western Europe has a capital remedy for a capital offense, forty of the states in the United States do.[9]

Consider, further, attitudes toward homosexuals and teaching. In Miami, Florida, in Minneapolis, Minnesota, and in Portland, Oregon, statutes that once permitted homosexuals to teach have been rescinded; in these communities homosexuals may not teach in elementary or secondary schools.[10] Whether one supports or rejects the new antihomosexual legislation, it is clearly a move in a less libertarian direction. It narrows rather than widens the range of vocational opportunity for certain citizens even though there is no empirical evidence that the presence of homosexual teachers in classrooms has deleterious effects on students.

Consider also the growing membership in fundamentalist religions. Since 1970 there has been a 15 percent increase in the membership of fundamentalist churches, and the trend does not seem to be abating.[11] People seem to be seeking a more solid rock upon which to stand, and religious fundamentalism, whether in the form of "cult membership" or membership in more traditional and legitimate church groups, seems to be one way to obtain it. In 1941, when Erich Fromm wrote *Escape from Freedom*,[12] he pointed out that freedom was not a virtue that everybody sought. Freedom was a heavy cross to bear, something that many people could not or would not endure. Dismayed, perhaps, by the excesses of the postwar Vietnam period, by the New Left, by what appears to be a breakdown in simple morality, by the increase in divorce, by the weakening of community life through increased family mobility, we seem to be seeking older, simpler, and more predictable ways; something to act as a counterbalance in a world in which we find it increasingly difficult to maintain our stability. Going "back to the basics" in education may be a further manifestation of this desire to return to a saner, less complex, and more familiar world.

The existence of this climate in the culture at large is supported by two other developments, both of which exacerbate the existing trend. One is the decrease in the school-age population. The other is the increase in the promise of technique.

Since 1972, the school-age population at the elementary level has declined about 10 percent.[13] At the secondary level the decline has been about 9 percent. This decline in student population has been accompanied by a reduction in the amount of money available to schools. Since approximately 80 percent of all states allocate funds to local school districts on the basis of average daily attendance, the drop in student enrollment has resulted in an absolute drop in the total amount of state funds that local school districts receive. Once funds are reduced, priorities must be articulated. It is no longer possible to continue to offer what has been offered. Reduction in student enrollment cannot be balanced by a corresponding reduction in lighting or heating, or even by turning off the ubiquitous Xerox machine. Some costs—lighting and heating, for example—are fixed regardless of the number of students that are enrolled, and, with fewer students, economies of volume are lost.

To reduce costs, savings must come from salaries, that portion which constitutes about 85 percent of the fiscal pie. Salaries must be cut, and people must be fired or not be reappointed. This requires that school boards define what they believe to be truly fundamental. In such a period, "innovation" is a word seldom to be heard. Once the watchword of Title III of the Elementary and Secondary Education Act in the 1960's, today it is the last word one is likely to hear falling from the lips of a school superintendent. At present the public has little taste for what it regards as frivolities. This is time for meat and potatoes, not soufflé.

The second development that has lent support to the current conservative educational climate is the promise of technique. The technique of which I speak is pedagogical. Since the early 1960s, American educationists, especially those in the behaviorist branches of psychology, have been particularly interested in developing the means to control and measure student behavior. If such means could be designed or "discovered" it would be possible to achieve in education the kinds of results possible in some areas of medicine and in many areas of engineering. Indeed, medicine and engineering are often used as paradigm fields by educational technologists, and terms such as "prescription," "diagnosis," "entry behavior," and "exit skills" are frequently heard in discourse about teaching.[14]

There is, of course, utility in using root metaphors for the analysis of teaching and education generally. Fresh metaphors, borrowed from other fields, often provide new perspectives on old problems, thereby making it possible to treat those problems in new ways. But metaphors —all metaphors, like all theories—also have a cost. That cost resides in the ways in which they shape our conception of the problems we study. And, because metaphors do not wear their values on their sleeves, we often unknowingly accept the values and assumptions embedded within them when we use them to study or explain educational practice. Thus, to talk about "diagnosis" in teaching leads quite naturally to conclusions about "prescription" and "treatment." To talk about "input" leads quite naturally to questions about "output." In addition, images accompany the metaphorical concepts. The images that have been salient in the educational research community have been largely industrial and technological.[15] They have been primarily concerned with the development and use of techniques for purposes of management and control. When a public is nervous about the efficacy of its schools, it tends to tighten up and to seek evidence concerning their productivity. For the educational research community, by and large, this has meant finding techniques that efficiently produce what is desired and using "objective" means for demonstrating the effectiveness of the technique chosen.

Perhaps one of the classic examples of the interest in technique was expressed in the desire to produce "teacherproof" curriculum materials. If one could design materials that even the most incompetent teacher could use successfully, it would virtually be possible to guarantee academic achievement. A belief in such a possibility was not rare in the middle part of the 1960s. American technology had produced a great deal: radar, a space capsule orbiting the earth, the landing of a man on the moon. If these complex tasks could be mastered by the marriage of science and technology, then why not reading, mathematics, and even social studies. The stumbling block in the minds of some curriculum developers was the teacher. It was the teacher who was the noise in the system, whose behavior one could not really depend upon. But if materials could be developed so that the unreliability of the teacher could be bypassed or overcome, the complete management of the learner's behavior and, hence, his achievement could be assured. In such a system the teacher would serve as an implementer of a scientifically developed technology of curriculum and instruction. American education sought efficacy by attempting to emulate the methods of those who put a man on the moon.

At one time, only a few years ago, the computer terminal was regarded as one of the most promising means to teach the young—if not poetry or art, then at least spelling and math. At one time, the use of a token economy in the classroom was believed to be one of the most promising tools for shaping desired student behavior. The promise of these techniques has begun to pale. While they are still used in some schools (students are paid 25¢ a day to attend some school in San Diego), the high expectations that were once held for them have been set at a more realistic level. Yet, the use of extrinsic reward systems as a technique for the management of problems whose roots go far beyond the surface still occurs too frequently in American schools.[16] Consider the use of such rewards in the schools of Dade County, Florida, a school district that, like many others, has a problem related to truancy. The administration in that district is trying to solve the problem this way:

> Trying to reduce the high absentee rates in the Dade Public Schools, officials have come up with a plan to entice truants into classrooms with gifts of frisbees, T-shirts, hamburgers, chicken dinners and yo-yos. The first attendance incentives donated by local businessmen will be handed out to students next month with the best attendance record at Brownsville Junior High School and Douglas Elementary School. Teachers with the best attendance rate in those schools will be rewarded with free gasoline, record albums and crab dinners. Robert Davidson, the school community liaison officer instrumental in starting the program said that other schools in the system are being encouraged to adopt similar programs.[17]

I do not believe that it takes much insight or professional training to recognize that, if the Dade Public Schools do indeed have an attendance problem, the problem is not likely to be resolved, either for students or teachers, by providing them with free chicken or crab dinners. One might well ask what schools teach the young when they use such techniques. It is too easy, when one focuses one's attention on the achievement of particular goals through the use of particular techniques, to neglect attending to the ancillary consequences of the techniques that one uses. It is the greatest of educational fallacies, Dewey said, to believe that children learn only one thing at a time.[18]

One serious problem with the preoccupation with the technical is the problem of neglecting the side effects that one produces en route to one's destination.[19] Within a technical framework, what matters most is getting where one wants to go; the character of the journey is less important. And when one is working in a cultural climate where the demand for results is great, the temptation to use whatever is expedient is even greater. In a time of educational crisis, it is not likely that one will have the "luxury" of attending to concomitant outcomes or to the consummatory aspects of educational experience. The goal is achievement, not inquiry. This preoccupation in American education is, of course, not a new one. With the decline of the progressive spirit in American education came a more goal-directed approach to practice—pragmatism writ small rather than large became the dominating perspective.

Twenty years ago Herbert Thelen, a professor of education at the University of Chicago, wrote:

> It is in the formulation of the problem that individuality is expressed, that creativity is stimulated, and that nuances and subtleties are discovered. It is these aspects of inquiry that give birth to new social movements and political orientations, and that are central in the emergence of insight. Yet it is precisely these aspects of inquiry that schools ignore, for they collapse inquiry to mere problem-solving, and they keep the student busy finding "solutions" to "problems" that are already formulated, externalized, depersonalized, and emotionally fumigated. The school is concerned with the student who formulates his own problems only when he is so creative with school property that he perforce enters a "counseling" relationship (on pain of dismissal). But as far as the academic work of the school goes, personal stirrings and strivings and self-discoveries have no place. In effect, what is missing is the investment of learning with personal emotion and meaning.[20]

The concerns Thelen expressed in 1960 are perhaps even more appropriate today.

Consequences for Schools

To paint a picture, as I have, of an America in the midst of a conservative mood and of its schools being chastised for having failed to achieve even mediocrity is not to imply that there are not schools, classrooms, administrators, and teachers that are not excellent in the best sense in which educational practice can be excellent. America is a large country. There are 45 million students attending about 100,000 schools, located in 16,000 school districts throughout the land. One can find in this country of ours everything from the very best by any set of educational standards to the very worst. What I have tried to paint is a general picture adumbrating a general set of trends that yield a general climate within most schools where administrators and teachers function. The specific consequences of this climate for the schools in general need to be considered.

One of the most significant consequences for the school that has resulted from the climate that prevails is the evisceration of the curriculum. There was a time when the concept of a balanced curriculum was much discussed. While it was never really clear what a balanced curriculum was, how far it extended, or even how one knew when one had one, the general belief that children needed opportunities to work in a variety of fields of study was an important one. Teachers could introduce the sciences and the arts with a clear educational conscience, firm in the belief that pupils ought not to be deprived of experience in these fields. Like the balanced diet, the balanced curriculum was believed to contribute to the educational health of the young. Not only that, there was also the general belief, particularly at the primary school level, that subjects should be taught in relation to one another, that disciplinary isolation was artificial, and that meaning was likely to be increased if pupils could use all of their senses in learning. An important aim was to help them see the interrelationships of, say, social studies and art, science and mathematics, language arts and social science.

Today the climate has changed. I do not know exactly what the average shift in time allocation is between what was provided to children fifteen years ago, field by field, and what is provided today. But fifteen years ago the provision of a balanced curriculum was a professional expectation, not a professional liability. The elementary schoolteacher who took her pupils on a field trip and then designed projects employing writing, math, social studies, art, music, and dramatics as a means to stimulate and guide learning was thought to be engaged in excellent teaching. It is questionable whether a teacher can afford to teach in such a manner today. Field trips are difficult to take in a period when insurance costs have skyrocketed and funds for buses have evaporated. And teaching the arts, except perhaps in the service of achieving better reading scores, is simply not regarded as the way one should spend one's time.

The neglect of those fields that were thought to constitute a balanced curriculum is supported by researchers who have done or reviewed research on what has come to be called "time on task."[21] Studies of time on task have revealed several things. First, the amount of time devoted to particular subjects in the curriculum is not equal. Some subjects receive ten to fifteen times as much attention as others. Second, a substantial proportion of the time that teachers spend in class is devoted to activities that have little to do with formal instruction: discipline problems and other forms of classroom management, for example.

Third, even those periods that are formally devoted to instruction, say, in math, do not always capture all of the student's attention. Thus, in every classroom there is a ratio between the time allocated to a particular subject and the time students actually concentrate on learning that subject. Fourth, the teacher working with pupils who are of lower socioeconomic status spends substantially more time on noninstructional activities than the teacher working with pupils who are of upper-middle socioeconomic status. Over the course of a year small differences in time allocated on a daily basis aggregate and become substantial. Finally, there is a positive significant relationship between the amount of time spent in a subject and the achievement of pupils in that subject.[22]

One conclusion that can be drawn from these studies is that attention to some fields of study, the arts, for example, is negatively correlated with pupil achievement in the three Rs. One writer reviewing studies of school achievement in academic subjects has this to say:

> The message of this section seems clear. The stronger the academic emphasis, the stronger the academic results. Time spent on reading and numbers is associated with growth in those areas, whereas time spent in other areas appears to detract from growth in reading and mathematics. Furthermore, there are *no* non-academic activities that yielded positive correlations with reading and mathematics achievement. This finding is somewhat surprising, since it has frequently been argued that some of these other activities contribute to reading achievement by motivating students or by providing additional stimulation or practice. Such indirect enhancement was not evident in this study.[23]

When one functions in a climate in which people are already concerned about student performance in the three Rs, findings such as these and the recommendations that researchers make can only exacerbate the move toward an unbalanced curriculum. Although a few years ago the debate on reading was over method—whether one should use phonics or the word-sight approach—today there is no comparable debate. The issue is essentially one of emphasis, and emphasis translates into more time.

When one calculates the amount of time devoted to certain fields of study at the elementary school level, one finds that on the average about 75 to 80 percent of all formal instructional time is devoted to the three Rs. If schools, as is claimed, have done such a poor job of teaching children to read, write, and compute when they spend this much time trying to do so, should they devote even more time to what is now being done so poorly? Is this another case of throwing good money after bad? Does one improve the quality of education by continuing to do what has not been effective in the first place?

But the problem of deciding what to teach goes beyond the question of whether to devote more time to instruction in the three Rs, even if one could guarantee that such instruction would be effective. The problem of deciding what to teach is not resolved by achieving highly prized goals related to a few important skills, but, rather, by grappling with questions related to the kinds of experience and opportunities for learning children should have. To suggest, as some researchers have, that more time should be devoted to reading instruction in order to raise test scores by a month or two is much too bald a prescription; it neglects the larger question of why current procedures are ineffective, and it fails to assess the potential costs of spending that most precious of resources, time, on a program that limits what children might otherwise have an opportunity to learn. If it is true, as the researchers on time on task have suggested, that children who are given an opportunity to learn X are more likely to learn it than children who are not, then clearly we should be as interested in what we are *not* giving children an opportunity to learn as we seem to be in what we do provide.

The overall consequences for the school curriculum and for the goals of schooling have been to constrict the range of fields to which children have access. So much elementary school teaching has been reduced to the three Rs that, when other types of learning activities are provided, they often have to be justified by their contribution to what is regarded as "the basics." But reduction of the curriculum to a limited conception of content is far from the only significant consequence of the current climate. Method has also been affected. If one is to be systematic about one's teaching, if one is to employ "fail-safe" procedures for instruction, it becomes important to develop or adapt a systematically oriented instructional system that is sequentially organized to ensure two things: pedagogical success and evidence of effectiveness. What this means for many teachers is the use of commercially developed instructional packages that break up complex skills into small steps so that each step can be taken one at a time. These packages also provide the teacher with tests that he or she can use to secure evidence of pupils' success in mastering each of the steps.[24]

The use of such an approach to teaching and learning is probably appropriate for some children most of the time and for all of the children some of the time. When such an approach becomes pervasive, however, there are significant liabilities. In the first place, the constant use of worksheets and tests can have the seductive and pernicious effect of leading children to believe that the most important reason for reading and doing math is to pass tests or to be able to hand in a completed worksheet. The use of these skills for purposes that go beyond the rewards and penalities of taking tests is easily neglected. Again, as Thelen suggested, achievement rather than inquiry is triumphant.[25] Even more disconcerting is the fact that many children learn to like the security that such procedures provide. The reduction of ambiguity and the security of knowing that one can always know when one is right or wrong is a seductive comfort in a world characterized by ambiguities, trade-offs, and dilemmas.

The use of a tight prescriptive curriculum structure, sequential skill development, and frequent testing and reward are classic examples of form becoming content. What pupils learn is not only a function of the formal and explicit content that is selected; it is also a function of the manner in which it is taught. The characteristics of the tasks and the tacit expectations that are a part of the structured program become themselves a part of the content.[26] In this sense teaching and curriculum merge. The distinction between the two as method and content will not hold once it is seen that the means that one employs itself defines the covert structure that embodies a significant part of what it is that students learn. Indeed, because the forms of teaching and classroom life generally are not framed as content, it is often difficult to appreciate the extent to which they shape what students learn in school.

The forms I speak of have been referred to as codes operating within a context that students learn during their time in school.[27] What are the characteristics of those codes in elementary and secondary schools at present? How have they changed during the past decade? To what extent do these codes differ for students of different socioeconomic status and educational ambition? And what kinds of attitudes and forms of thinking do those codes most salient in classrooms tend to develop? Inquiry into such questions would require a far broader approach to the evaluation of learning than is usually undertaken to assess student achievement. The very limited information that standard forms of evaluation provide may seriously distort our perception of the reality that we are trying to understand and improve.

While this reduction in the scope of school curricula is occurring, there is at the same time a move to expand the concept of education so that it includes *all* forms of learning fostered by the culture. As a concept, education becomes equated with socialization and learning. While it is clearly the case that schools have no monopoly on the educational process, it is in my view unwise to blur the distinction between learning and education. Not everything that is learned is educational: some things learned are miseducational. Learning to feel fearful and incompetent, learning to become a bigot, and learning to become dependent are only a few. While it is prudent to remind ourselves that the educational process can occur in principle whenever individuals have intercourse with the world, it is a mistake to regard all forms of learning as synonomous with education. Learning can diminish the mind as well as expand it.

Although these two views, one reductionist and the other expansionist, appear at first to be at opposite poles, they in fact support each other. If education is viewed as a process identical to learning and if one then argues that every social institution—the home, the church, the factory, the office—educates, it no longer becomes critical for the school to try to do all of the things that it once attempted. Many of those things will be done outside of the school. Therefore, the argument proceeds, let the school do what only the school can do; let it concentrate on reading, writing, and arithmetic, and on those other formal academic content areas that social institutions outside the school are not likely to teach.[28] An expanded view of the sources of educational experience is easily used as an argument to reduce the scope of the school curriculum.

Any description of the factors contributing to the prevailing climate in American education must include a discussion of the impact of the testing and accountability movement. Although a great deal of conceptual sophistication has been achieved in the field of educational evaluation over the past decade, these developments have not, by and large, taken root in the mainstream of American schools. Approaches to evaluation that are "goal free,"[29] "illuminative,"[30] "ethnomethodological,"[31] "qualitative,"[32] "responsive,"[33] and the like are largely approaches that are described in the articles published in professional journals, in doctoral dissertations, and in papers delivered at professional meetings. While the odd school- or school district-based project might employ one or more of these approaches to evaluation, in the main American schools do not.

What schools in general do employ are state-mandated standardized achievement tests designed to provide the public with evidence of their effectiveness. In California, for example, standardized achievement tests are administered to all students at least once in grades 4 and 6, once in grades 7 and 9, and twice in grades 10 and 11.[34] In Michigan, students in grades 4 and 7 are tested. In New Mexico, students are tested by the state in grades 5, 8, and 11. In New Jersey, the mandate prescribes that students in grades 3, 6, 9, and 11 be tested.[35] In Washington and Wisconsin, students in grades 4, 8, and 11 are tested. These states are by no means exceptional. As of December 1979, thirty-eight of the fifty-two states had developed or had plans to develop and implement statewide testing programs.[36]

There can be no doubt that the use of tests, particularly when their results are made public, do considerably more than describe the state of educational affairs. Testing programs not only describe, they prescribe. The way in which prescription occurs is by shedding some light on some aspects of human performance while neglecting other aspects. If the test that is used is norm referenced, it has been *designed* to yield a normal distribution of scores, in which case about half of all students taking the test will perform below the average. In American society no one wants to be below average, regardless of the magnitude of the mean. Thus, tests become one of the most potent tools for shaping educational priorities because their public use focuses public attention not only on some aspects of student achievement while neglecting others, but also because they highlight those students who score below average. Out of the normal distribution of scores are born educational needs: 50 percent of the students taking the test will be below the mean, and about 25 percent will be in the lowest quartile. It is a rare community that is able, on its own, to interpret the results of testing programs adequately. And when test scores by school and grade are published in rank order in local newspapers, as they are in many communities, it is the rare school principal who can easily tolerate his or her school being at the lower end of the continuum.

It is not difficult to understand what teachers have come to feel about the use and consequences of testing. Few are happy with testing programs. The Elementary School Principals' Association has devoted two complete issues of its journal to the liabilities of testing, one to achievement testing and the other to intelligence testing.[37] Yet few teachers or administrators can afford to ignore the consequences of their use. In practice, this means that even teachers whose philosophic commitment is to a wide view of curriculum often cannot afford to devote time to those fields that are not tested. A weak program that is not tested may seldom come to light; those areas that are tested will.

There are, of course, positive uses for tests in and out of schools. Tests are often highly efficient means for securing information that would otherwise be very time consuming and expensive to obtain. Because the same test can be administered to many people, it is possible to compare the scores of individuals and groups and to use those scores as a basis for the prediction of performance. Most standardized achievement tests yield scores that predict performance on tasks similar to those tested far better than would otherwise be possible. Yet tests are limited by the technology that gives rise to them. Even if one is given certain criteria as standards against which to validate or appraise a test, there are many significant educational goals that are not easily tested: the desire to continue to learn what one has been taught, for example. What is not easily tested is frequently neglected. What is easy to test, at least comparatively, is more likely to be tested. The differential in the kinds of information made available to the public as a function of what is and what is not tested significantly affects the priorities of schools. One of the most effective ways to create an educational crisis is to develop a norm-referenced achievement test, administer it widely, and attach significant social consequences to the results. One would soon find that about half of the students taking this test were deficient and that those in the first quartile were having serious difficulty. In all likelihood, this would bring about a stream of newspaper and magazine articles lambasting the schools for their fecklessness and demanding that the newfound defects be remedied by giving them more attention in school. Soon a new educational need would emerge.

This flow of events from test scores to educational goals is, of course, the reverse of the textbook version of how tests should be used in educational practice. The standard version prescribes that one first establish objectives, then design a series of curriculum activities related to those objectives, then implement these activities through teaching, and, finally, test or in other ways evaluate to determine if the goals that were initially formulated have been achieved. The direction is from goals to test data as a means of checking effectiveness. In the operation of schools the reverse trend is more common. Goals are abstractions. What students want to know is not what the goals of the program are, but how they will be evaluated. Teachers, like the rest of us, are no different. We can afford to neglect the laudable abstractions represented in goal statements, but few of us can afford to neglect the social and personal consequences of poor test scores. Learning what counts in social situations is one of the survival skills of social life, and the lessons are learned quite early.

Another consequence of large-scale, state-mandated testing programs is that their use tends to reduce the school's prerogatives for establishing its own priorities. When the locus of control emanates from the results of test performance and when a school, a principal, or a teacher is judged by the scores their students achieve on tests, neither the school, the principal, nor the teacher retains the initiative regarding the particular priorities suitable for the students they serve. The teacher and the principal clearly relinquish some of their professional autonomy by the constraints that test scores impose. When judgments about educational quality are made on the basis of test performance, not only is the scope of the curriculum likely to be diminished, but the climate for educational innovation is also likely to be dampened.

This diminution of the scope for choice at the local level is another of the paradoxes of American education. We live in a period in which there has seldom been a greater desire for local participation in the formation of educational policy. In 1974 New York City established thirty-eight local school boards within its seven boroughs in order to accommodate the growing public expectation that it, the public, has the right to form and review educational policy.[38] In California the concept of School Site Councils was created in order to increase the policy-making options of the community near each school. While these moves to increase local control are occurring, the increase in statewide testing programs and the increase in the state funding of schools is also occurring. On the one hand, California moved from funding about 40 percent, on the average, of the budgets of local school districts in 1976 to 63 percent in 1979.[39] On the other hand, in the state that has increased by over 50 percent its fiscal contribution to local school districts, the voucher plan is being seriously considered as a way of giving parents greater choice in the schools their children will attend. In the meantime, teachers protect their own professional interests through unionization or by leaving teaching for more fertile and satisfying fields elsewhere.

The use of test data as a means of judging the quality of schools gains a great deal of support from colleges and universities that use test results as one of the bases for student admission. The Scholastic Aptitude Test is a major example. Each year about 1.5 million high school students take the SATs as a part of the dossier that they will submit to the college of their choice.[40] Although college admission officers claim that the weight of SAT scores is overestimated by students, the reality for students, teachers, and administrators alike is that they believe that the scores are important, so important that many high schools have created specific courses to help students acquire high scores on the test. Time that might have been used to deal with problems or fields of genuine substantive interest to students is devoted to the task of learning how to answer questions on a test that the student believes will significantly affect his or her chances for college admission, but which otherwise has little intrinsic value.

When one examines the Scholastic Aptitude Test, one finds that it has two sections: one devoted to the assessment of verbal aptitude; the other, of mathematical aptitude. It becomes clear to students, or so they believe, that the likelihood of achieving high scores in these sections will be increased if they do additional coursework in English and mathematics. Even students whose interests and aptitudes reside in other subjects relinquish the opportunity to pursue those interests in order to avoid jeopardizing their chances for college admission in a competitive academic world. Many students select courses primarily with an eye on those abilities they know they will have to display on the test rather than because they are interested in what the courses teach. They come to believe that they must pay their dues in the present in order to have the kind of future that they desire. Again, discussion about laudable and expansive educational aims pales when compared to the reality of how students will be evaluated.

But the legitimation of certain human abilities through the use of the SAT is not the only means through which universities shape curriculum priorities for college-bound students. Some do it through formal notices sent to American secondary schools about what they require of aspiring entrants while others do it through formally prescribed course requirements and through policies that assign different weights to grades received in particular courses. A vivid example of the former is the brochure sent to 10,000 secondary schools by the Undergraduate Committee on Admission and Financial Aid at Stanford University.[41] The brochure that was sent to these schools was motivated by the belief among members of the admission committee that secondary school standards had fallen, that grade inflation had rendered grades largely meaningless, and that students who were intellectually able did not have sufficient work in really difficult secondary school courses. To remedy this state of affairs, examples of four high school programs were provided in the brochure. These sample programs were arrayed from "solid" to what might be regarded, I suppose, as "liquid." The program of study reflecting the most "solid" characteristics contained eight subjects that were taken simultaneously during the first semester of the tenth grade and eight subjects taken during the second semester. Among those subjects was a course in German, one in Greek, one in Latin, a laboratory science, English, a course in advanced algebra, one in U.S. history, and one in Chinese history. The least solid program contained no work in a foreign language and courses in band and art. The brochure, in both its prose and its sample programs, left little doubt as to what Stanford's Committee on Undergraduate Admission and Financial Aid considered intellectually demanding. Although claiming that it was not the committee's intention to influence the character of secondary school curricula, it is difficult to see how any other effect could be achieved.

The University of California system—all nine campuses—prescribes similar requirements and, like Stanford, clearly indicates that grades received in some areas of study, the arts, for example, will not be taken into account in calculating the student's grade point average.[42] Thus, a student who wants to pursue work in the arts and at the same time wants to be admitted to Stanford or to the University of California system has something of a dilemma. By enrolling in arts courses, the student faces double jeopardy. He or she raises the admission committee's suspicion that he is fearful of the so-called really difficult subjects and, at the same time, he forgoes the opportunity to raise the level of his grade point average by taking courses where the grades are ignored when calculating that average.

Policies such as these both legitimate and reinforce a particular conception of mind. Although developed with good intentions by well-meaning faculty members, such policies, from the prestigious position from which they emanate, sanction what students shall study. They provide easy answers to questions of curriculum content, and they reinforce the uneasy feeling that many citizens experience that schools have badly wandered from doing what is really important.

Thus, it is not difficult to recognize that the so-called "back to basics" movement within American education is a part of a more general cultural development. Our attitudes toward schools are a part of a larger, more general conservative attitude, one that manifests itself in policies regarding who shall be permitted to teach, who shall live and who shall be executed, who shall secure financial support for social services, and who shall go without. It manifests itself in policies concerning the busing of school children, in the public's willingness to cut resources for public services, and in the growing desire to find better and more secure answers than have been provided in the past regarding the ways in which one should live one's life.

These developments in the nation at large, as we have seen, are not without their contradictions. Local control of the schools is being called for, while, at the same time, statewide prescriptive testing policies are being implemented. The voucher plan for schools may be on the California ballot in 1984, while the state is significantly increasing the percentage of its fiscal contributions to local school districts. The range of curricular content and the scope of educational goals are being narrowed at the very time that the concept of education is being expanded.

Such contradictory developments are not surprising. Contradiction and paradox are more characteristic of educational debate and practice in the United States than quiet uniformity. There is no Minister of Education comparable to those found in most countries of the world. Differences in views about schooling are protected—in some places cherished. Yet, after having said that, it is undeniable that the pervasive characteristic of school policy and practice in the latter part of the 1970's and the early 1980's has been, and is likely to be, one that is more conservative than liberal, one that looks back as much as it looks forward, one that cherishes older values more than it seeks new ones.

Meeting the Challenge

If one accepts a functional theory of social behavior, each of the policies enacted and each of the practices employed serve some useful purpose. If a society seeks stability, the policies and programs it adopts are likely to be motivated by such a desire. Yet functionalism can be used to justify any move. Educational practice is a value-oriented enterprise and educators have a normative, not just a technical, role to play in education. We do not have to content ourselves with a socially deterministic view of schooling. We can, both as professionals and citizens, try to shape the kind of future that we want for our children, our society, and ourselves. This requires, of course, making commitments that are value oriented. It means taking a position without becoming dogmatic. Unfortunately, many school administrators feel so professionally vulnerable that they avoid expressing a view on educational aims, and those who are not professionally vulnerable, that is, tenured university professors of education, are often so committed to something that might be best described as "technical neutrality" that they have little interest in questions regarding the content of the curriculum and the goals of education. While studies might be made of the amount of time allocated to what is taught, these studies are undertaken as a descriptive activity, not as work that might explicitly reflect some value position on educational practice. The vulnerability of school administrators and the technical neutrality of university professors of education, particularly those who do research, has left a virtual vacuum of educational leadership in the United States.[43] Indeed, normative views of education, regardless of how well written, how penetrating, how incisive, would not be printed on the pages of the *American Educational Research Journal*. They would not be regarded as research.

Symptomatic of the emphasis on the technical is the growing tendency to call school principals and superintendents "educational managers," thus implying, further, that their role is not one of leadership but one that is essentially technical.[44] As teachers' unions become increasingly active and demanding, the skills of arbitration become more important in the training of administrators. To achieve these skills, an increasing number of courses are taken in schools of business and departments of economics. Work in the philosophy of education, courses in curriculum studies, programs in teaching and supervision are forgone in order to secure the technical skills university faculties believe prospective school administrators need in order to survive. What models of educational practice are possible, what their respective strengths and weaknesses are, what the varieties of excellent teaching look like, and how one might build an effective school community are questions that are seldom raised. Thus, the acquiescence of school administrators and teachers to practices and policies that they do not believe in—often without a word of dissent or discussion—is a tacit legitimation of the views of education that the public holds. When a school superintendent can keep his views of education hidden from the community after five years in the superintendency, there is a lack of professional leadership in the system.

Students pay the price for a reduced conception of education and a diminished curriculum. They take what they are offered because neither they nor their parents are in a position to know what they are not receiving. Not having the experience to know what the alternatives are, they adapt to what they find in school. What is even more disconcerting is that many come to prefer their lack of choice. A system with few real options often breeds a sense of security.

I, for one, believe that educators have a profound responsibility to perform more than a technical role in the school system. Technical competence is admittedly one of the sources of professional authority; knowing how to do a job is clearly what the public employs educators for. Yet, not to know what jobs are worth doing or to know but not to speak is a serious form of professional dereliction. The usual argument against educators performing a normative role as professionals within the school system takes the form that the norms to which schools are directed should be determined by the community, that such goals should be the result of political debate, that the professional's responsibility is to use the skills needed to realize the goals that have been formulated, that the professional has a right to participate in the formulation of goals for schools, but as a citizen and not as a professional educator.

I believe such a view of professional responsibility is far too limited, if for no other reason than because it denies the public access to the more studied views concerning educational ends that the educator should possess. If the educator's views of educational ends and the probable consequences of particular curriculum policies are no better informed than those of the public, then, of course, his claim to expertise is no stronger than theirs. But if this is so, it suggests that the level of professional competence is too low.

Matters such as these are fraught with controversy. Let me be clear about the role I see for the professional educator regarding the aims toward which curricula are directed. First, I believe that, because of their training, educators—teachers as well as school administrators—have a responsibility to appraise educational ends, as well as to employ technical skills related to achieving those ends. Second, I believe that the professional educator has a responsibility to help community groups making or influencing educational policy consider the alternatives to the ends to which they might currently subscribe. Such an appraisal should examine the potential costs as well as the potential benefits of particular kinds of programs. Third, while the ultimate policy-making body shaping the character and direction of school programs should be the lay community, the educator can and ought to exercise a leadership role in guiding the direction policy takes. This view neither suggests nor implies that educators should function in an authoritarian or dictatorial manner. In most communities such behavior would not be tolerated even if an educator wanted to function in that way. What it does mean is that the educator should articulate possible directions and state his or her reasons for preferring particular ones. There can be no educational leadership without followers; a community can always accept or reject the guidance that is being provided. Without acknowledgement that such a role is legitimate, however, the likelihood of professional leadership is diminished, and the professional role is reduced to that of technical hired hand who is simply expected to know how to get the job done. That role alone is not enough.

The position that I have taken regarding the role of the educator as educational leader rests upon the assumption that educators have reflected upon the questions of what ends are worth pursuing in the schools and what programs are instrumental to their realization. It rests upon the assumption that those who teach or administer schools understand something about how particular fields of study contribute to the intellectual development of the young and how programs can be created that encourage such development. It is to this area of educational theory that this small book is addressed. Thus far, I have tried to describe the context in which the schools function, to identify some of the forces that have shaped their contours, and to suggest that educators perform a leadership role within the educational system. To do that effectively requires an understanding of the ways in which educational programs can be conceptualized and evaluated. What follows is an effort to describe the forms of thought through which conceptualization in general occurs and the means humans use to represent what they have conceptualized to others. It is my conviction that efforts to revise curriculum and to develop new and more effective methods of educational evaluation need to be grounded in a view of how humans construct meaning from their experience. It is to these issues that we now turn our attention.

Notes

1. *Time Magazine*, June 16, 1980, p. 54.

2. Annegret Harnischfeger and David E. Wiley, *Achievement Test Score Decline: Do We Need to Worry?* Chicago: CEMREL, 1975, p. 139. Each year "more than a million" high school juniors and seniors take the SATs (Advisory Panel on the Scholastic Aptitude Test Score Decline, *On Further Examination*, New York: College Entrance Examination Board, 1977, p. 1); in 1977, there were 1,401,900 juniors, seniors, and repeaters who took the SATs (*ibid.*, p. 4); in 1974 there were 985,000 students (probably seniors) who took the SATs.

3. Between 1963 and 1977 there was a decline of 49 points in the average score on the verbal part of the SAT; 31 points on the math part. Advisory Panel . . ., *On Further Examination*, p. 5.

4. Declines have also occurred in the ACT (American College Testing Program), the MSAT (Minnesota Scholastic Aptitude Test), the NAEP (National Assessment of Educational Progress), and on the CTBS (Comprehensive Tests of Basic Skills) for grades 5 to 10, but *not* for grades 2 to 4. Harnischfeger and Wiley, *Achievement Test Score Decline*, pp. 1–4.

5. The University of the Pacific offers students aid in developing basic reading and writing skills at their learning assistance center. San Francisco State offers a similar "developmental" program, dealing with a range of needs from "very low skills in writing" to "students wishing improvement." *Source*: Learning Assistance Center, San Francisco State University. Foothill College offers tutorial assistance to "many students" who lack basic reading and writing skills for completing basic course assignments. They also have a developmental learning assistance program and tutors for foreign students. *Source*: Learning Assistance Center, Foothill Junior College. "It would be fair to assert that universities have broadened their learning assistance services (in reading, writing, math, and study skills) in response to a *feeling* that performance is declining in the lower grades; although the cause-effect relationship is not entirely clear here." *Source*: Carolyn Walker, Director, Stanford Learning Assistance Center, interview. One of the major motivations for broadening the services of the Learning Assistance Center at Stanford University in 1972 was the feeling that a more diverse pool of applicants required special assistance. Harvard University and the University of California, Berkeley, also have such centers. *Source*: Carolyn Walker, "The Learning Assistance Center in a Selective Institution," in *New Directions for College Learning Assistance*, San Francisco: Jossey-Bass, 1980.

6. In 1972 the United States Supreme Court handed down the landmark decision, *Forman* v. *Georgia*, on capital punishment. It ruled that the death penalty was "cruel and unusual punishment" because it did not conform to minimum standards of retributive justice; specifically, because administration of the death penalty has been "rare, arbitrary, and discriminatory." The majority supported its decision with statistics on discrimination in the application of capital punishment. William J. Bowers, *Executions in America*, Lexington, Mass.: Lexington Books, 1974, pp. xix–xxi.

7. Bowers (*ibid.*) offers support to the assertion that the death penalty has been racially discriminatory. "There is no doubt that capital punishment has functioned in a racially discriminatory fashion, especially for the crime of rape" (p. xix). Of rape offenders, nonwhites have been executed at a rate six times (18.6% as opposed to 2.5%) that of whites (p. 77).

8. *Ibid.*, p. xix. By the end of 1973 "nearly two dozen" states had reinstated capital punishment, with similar legislation pending in a dozen others.

9. A table (*ibid.*) lists the abolition of the death penalty for every country in Western Europe except Spain.

10. The United States Supreme Court upheld the dismissal in 1972 of James Gaylord, who had been teaching in the Tacoma School District for twelve years, solely because he admitted that he was a homosexual. No evidence of immoral conduct or of a detrimental effect on his teaching was presented. James J. Flygare, "Supreme Court Refuses to Hear Case of Discharged Homosexual Teacher," *Phi Delta Kappan*, 59: 482–483, March 1978.

11. *Yearbook of American and Canadian Churches*, Nashville: Abingdon Press, n.d.

12. Erich Fromm, *Escape from Freedom*, New York: Farrar and Rinehart, 1941.

13. Harriet Fishlow, "Demography and Changing Enrollments," unpublished manuscript, School Finance and Organization Symposium, 1976.

14. Articles on prescriptive-diagnostic approaches to teaching have appeared in *The Education Index* with the following frequency:

1979–80:	18	1976–77:	18
1978–79:	18	1975–76:	19
1977–78:	23	1974–75:	22

An overview of this approach is provided by John Stellern *et al.*, *Introduction to Diagnostic-Prescriptive Teaching and Programming*, Golden Ridge, N. J.: Exceptional Press, 1976.

15. Ernest House, "Coherence and Credibility: The Aesthetics of Evaluation," *Educational Evaluation and Policy Analysis*, 1:5–17, September-October 1979.

16. Mark R. Lepper, ed., *The Hidden Cost of Reward*, Hillsdale, N. J.: Erlbaum Associates, 1978.

17. *Miami Herald*, October 24, 1977.

18. John Dewey, *Experience and Education*, New York: Macmillan, 1938.

19. These side effects are often considered the main effects in schooling, particularly by writers concerned with educational equity and self-esteem.

20. Herbert Thelen, *Education and the Human Quest*, New York: Harper, 1960.

21. See, for example, T. L. Good and T. M. Beckerman, "Time on Task: A Naturalistic Study in Sixth-Grade Classrooms," *Elementary School Journal*, 78:192–201, January 1978; B. V. Rosenshine, "Academic Engaged Time, Content Covered, and Direct Instruction," *Journal of Education*, 160:38–66, August 1978.

22. Rosenshine, "Academic Engaged Time."

23. Barak Rosenshine, "Classroom Instruction," in *Psychology of Teaching Methods*, 75th Yearbook of the National Society for the Study of Education, Part I, ed. N. L. Gage, Chicago: University of Chicago Press, p. 345.

24. Siegfried Engelman, *Distar Reading I, II, and III: An Instructional System*, Chicago: Science Research Associates.

25. Thelen, *Education and the Human Quest*.

26. This is what is referred to in the literature as "the hidden curriculum."

27. Ulf Lundgren and Sten Pattersson, eds., *Code, Context and Curriculum Processes*, Lund: Liberlømaromede/Gleerup, 1979.

28. Carl Bereiter, *Must We Educate?* Englewood Cliffs, N. J.: Prentice-Hall, 1974.

29. Michael Scriven, "Goal-Free Evaluation," in *Beyond the Numbers Game*, ed. David Hamilton *et al.*, Berkeley, Calif.: McCutchan, 1977.

30. See, especially, Hamilton *et al.*, *Beyond the Numbers Game*.

31. Frederick Erickson, "Some Approaches to Inequity in School-Community Ethnography," *Anthropology and Education Quarterly*, 8:58–68, February 1977.

32. Elliot W. Eisner, *The Educational Imagination: On the Design and Evaluation of Educational Programs*, New York: Macmillan, 1979.

33. Robert E. Stake, *Evaluating Educational Programs*, Washington, D. C.: Organization for Economic Cooperation and Development Publications Center, 1976.

34. In California progress toward proficiency standards are assessed at least once from grades 4 to 6, once from grades 7 to 9, and twice in grades 10 and 11. *Source*: *Technical Assistance Guide for Proficiency Assessment*, Sacramento: California State Department of Education, 1977, p. 1. In New Jersey there is statewide testing in grades 3, 6, 9, and 11. *Source*: *Compendium of Educational Research, Planning, Evaluation and Assessment Activities*, Trenton: New Jersey Department of Education, 1977, p. 86. Other statewide testing schedules listed in New Jersey's *Compendium* are: Michigan, grades 4, 7 (p. 67); New Mexico, grades 5, 8, 11 (p. 87); Washington, grades 4, 8, 11 (p. 130); Wisconsin, grades 4, 8, 12 (p. 132); Rhode Island, grades 4, 8 (p. 227). As of 1977, North Carolina, Idaho, and Alaska were developing statewide tests.

35. New Jersey's *Compendium*.

36. In 1973 there were statewide assessment programs in 33 states. Educational Resource Information Center, *State Testing Programs*, Princeton, N. J.: Educational Testing Service, 1973, p. 1.

37. *National Elementary Principal*, 54: entire issue, March-April 1975 (IQ testing); 54: entire issue, July-August 1975 (standardized achievement testing).

38. New York City has 32 local elementary school boards, 5 high school boards, and 1 special school board. *Directory of Public Schools and Administrators*, Albany: New York State Education Department, 1978, pp. 58–60.

39. Between 1974 and 1979 California state support for local school districts increased from 40% to 63%. This will probably increase further for 1980. *Source*: California State Board of Education, interview.

40. Advisory Panel . . . , *On Further Examination*.

41. Stanford University distinguishes between solid and nonsolid courses in its memo on exemplary high school programs. Office of Admission, Stanford University, "A Memo to Secondary Schools, Students, and Parents," October 1978.

42. The University of California requires the following courses in its evaluation of a high school transcript:

U.S. History	(1 year)	Foreign language	(2 years) and
English	(4 years)	one advanced course in math, a
Math	(2 years)	foreign language, or a lab science
Lab science	(1 year)		

Source: Office of Admissions, University of California, Berkeley.

43. Raymond Callahan, *Education and the Cult of Efficiency*, Chicago: University of Chicago Press, 1962.

44. For references to educational administrators as managers, see, for example, National Association of Secondary School Principals, *Management Crisis: A Solution*, Washington, D. C.: the Association, 1971; R. W. Hostrup, *Managing Education for Results*, Homewood, Ill.: ETC Publishing, 1975.

2

The Role of the Senses in Concept Formation

The aims of schooling and the development of the student's ability to think and to know have long been associated. Indeed, if there is any general educational goal to which both professional educators and the lay public subscribe, it is in what the literature refers to as "cognitive development."[1] The focus on the development of cognition as an educational goal is, I believe, quite appropriate; schools as institutions and education as a process ought to foster the student's ability to understand the world, to deal effectively with problems, and to acquire wide varieties of meaning from interactions with it. The development of cognition is the primary means to these ends. But just what is cognition, and what is not? What constitutes cognitive activity, and what kinds of activities are noncognitive? Unfortunately, cognition is often narrowly conceived.[2] Perhaps nowhere does this problem stand out more clearly than when cognition is contrasted with affect. Affect is supposed to deal with feeling and not with knowing, while cognition supposedly deals with knowing and not with feeling.

If such distinctions were simply theoretical conveniences, they might not cause as much practical mischief. The mischief stems from the fact that the distinctions are reified and practically applied. The cognitive and the affective are all too often regarded as distinct and independent states of the human organism. Such distinctions manifest themselves educationally in decisions that are made about the content of the curriculum and when aspects of that content shall be taught. Cognitive studies, those studies that require one to think should, it follows, be taught when students are fresh and alert since thinking, as contrasted with feeling, is demanding. Hence, subjects regarded as cognitive are taught in the morning, while those that are believed to be affective—the fine arts, for example—are taught (if at all) in the afternoon, often at the end of the week.[3] What happens is that the limited view of cognition that permeates so much psychological and educational literature legitimates a form of educational practice that itself limits what children have the opportunity to learn in school. Consider its impact on the use of time in school.

Observations about the importance of time in learning have already been made in the previous chapter. Time on task is the study of that relationship, and research in this area indicates that time is differentially allocated to different areas of study. The absolute amount of time devoted to particular subjects is not, however, the only factor that influences what children learn. *When* subjects are taught is also important. Thus, because some subjects are not only given the lion's share of attention but also given "prime time," decisions that are made about the use of time in the curriculum not only affect the student's access to particular content, they also convey to students what is regarded as important and what is not. If it was true that some subjects were noncognitive and if one believed that schools should emphasize the development of cognitive ability, one could make a case for allocating prime time to content areas that were cognitive. This case cannot be made because the hard and fast distinction between what is cognitive and what is affective is itself faulty. In the first place there can be no affective activity without cognition. If to cognize is to know, then to have a feeling and not to know it is not to have it. At the very least, in order to have a feeling one must be able to distinguish between one state of being and another. The making of this distinction is the product of thinking, a product that itself represents a state of knowing.

Similarly, there can be no cognitive activity that is not also affective.[4] Even if it were possible to think in a way that was void of feeling, such a state could be known only by knowing the feeling that the absence of feeling signifies. Although this appears to be paradoxical, it is not. To experience thought as bland, dull, boring, feckless—in short, as feelingless—is to recognize its feelingful character. When one's cognitive processes are permeated by other feeling tones, other affective qualities are obviously at work. In short, affect and cognition are not independent processes; nor are they processes that can be separated. They interpenetrate just as mass and weight do. They are part of the same reality in human experience.

Toward a Wider View of Cognition

My purpose in emphasizing the interdependence of cognition and affect is to illuminate the theoretical tradition that pervades our beliefs about human thought and to illustrate a few of the ways in which that tradition affects school curricula. A view of cognition that restricts thinking and knowing to forms of mentation that are exclusively discursive or mathematical leaves out far more than it includes. When such a conception then becomes extended so that human intelligence itself is defined by operations employing only, or even mainly, those forms of thinking, the liabilities of the view for education are multiplied even further. On this matter, John Dewey had some important things to say. Speaking of the relationship of intelligence to art, a so-called affective area, Dewey wrote:

> Any idea that ignores the necessary role of intelligence in production of works of art is based upon identification of thinking with use of one special kind of material, verbal signs and words. To think effectively in terms of relations of qualities is as severe a demand upon thought as to think in terms of symbols, verbal and mathematical. Indeed, since words are easily manipulated in mechanical ways, the production of a work of genuine art probably demands more intelligence than does most of the so-called thinking that goes on among those who pride themselves on being "intellectuals."[5]

Dewey's views were published in 1934 in a book that he wrote when he was more than seventy years old. *Art as Experience* is one of the last major works of his career, and yet it is largely unread in educational and psychological circles. The wide view of cognition that it portrays somehow never took root in mainstream educational or psychological theory.

What would a wider view of cognition look like? What would it suggest for the curriculum of the school and for educational evaluation? What new forms of intelligence might be recognized through it? What abilities would surface as children now regarded as nonintellectual became appreciated? How might such a view alter the kinds of questions that are now raised and studied concerning human abilities?

It should be remembered that the tendency to regard cognition as something independent of both "sense data" and feeling has a long history.[6] Plato regarded knowledge that was dependent on the senses as untrustworthy and believed affect to be a seductive distraction that kept man from knowing the truth.[7] Only pure thought unencumbered by feeling and by sense data could make it possible to know what was true.

Episteme—the Greek term for knowledge—was the result of a rational, not an empirical, process. Mathematics and dialectics were its foremost vehicles since both depended upon the use of "pure" reason.[8] The tendency to separate the cognitive from the affective is reflected in our separation of the mind from the body, of thinking from feeling, and the way we have dichotomized the work of the head from the work of the hand. What might seem at first to be abstract distinctions that have little bearing upon the real world in which we live turn out to shape not only our conception of mind but our educational policies as well. Students who are good with their hands might be regarded as talented, but seldom as intelligent. Those who are emotive, sensitive, or romantic might have aptitudes for the arts, but the "really bright" go into mathematics or the sciences. In some states those who are considered "intelligent," as defined by their IQ, receive state funds to enhance their educational development.[9] Those who are merely "talented" do not. Such distinctions in policy and in theory do not, in my view, do justice either to the children or to the society. More suitable curriculum policy might be formulated by appealing to a wider conception of mind and by formulating educational programs that are designed to expand its power. The place one might begin to develop a wider conception of mind is by examining the function of the senses and identifying the role they play in the achievement of mind.

All biological organisms possess means through which they establish contact with the environment. Even a single-cell amoeba is able to respond to and incorporate the life-sustaining resources that come into its midst. The human organism has, of course, an extraordinarily more varied sensory apparatus for making contact with the world. Each of the sensory systems is constructed to pick up information about some, but not all, of the qualities that constitute the immediate environment.[10] Thus, the organism's visual sensory system is designed to be sensitive to light. Given a normally functioning visual system, the organism has the capacity to discriminate among the qualities that constitute the visual world and to use the data secured to make inferences about it. The capacity of the human organism to differentiate among the qualities of the environment, to recall them in memory, and to manipulate them in the imagination is biologically rooted. As long as the particular sensory systems the human possesses are intact, the individual can learn how to differentiate, to recall, and to manipulate the qualities he encounters. Furthermore, the extent to which the sensory systems can be used to distinguish among those qualities to which they are biologically sensitive depends at least in part on the organism's prior experience and developmental history. For example, the four-week-old infant must learn how to focus and how to track moving objects,[11] but so must the forty-year-old adult who is first learning how to hunt. While the adult has all of the physiological prerequisites, other necessary conditions—prior hunting experience, for example—may be missing. As for the infant, *both* the physiological and the experiential conditions that are lacking will soon be gained, for, at about the age of four months, both the ability to focus and to track are well-developed skills in the normal child.

But imagine for a moment the situation if a child were congenitally blind or for some reason unable to secure tactile sensation. Suppose that child had never experienced light and that even its tongue was insensitive to tactile quality. What could the child know about the visual or the tactile? What could it remember of those qualities? To what extent could it create through its imagination what it had never had an opportunity to experience? There is no reason to believe that anything in these dimensions of experience could be secured. Consider an analogy.

Suppose we assume for a moment that each of us reading these pages was required from birth to wear red filters over our eyes. What, under such conditions, could we come to know of the colors of the environment? What would we make of our experience? What would we know about what we were unable to see? It would be difficult even to make inferences about this loss since we would not know what we had missed. Without access to what fully functioning sight provides, we would be unable even to speculate upon the character or magnitude of our loss.

Most of us assume, of course, that, by and large, we can experience most of what the world has to offer. Most of us have our senses intact, and in varying degrees we have learned to use them. Indeed, our conception of the world does not exceed what our senses have made possible. Even the smallest subparticle of the atom and the black holes of space, phenomena that no one has ever seen, are imaginable, visually illustrated or illustratable. Through imagination—the creation of mental images—we are able to conceive what we have never experienced in the empirical world.

The contribution of vision to conception and imagination are not contributions limited to vision alone. Each of the sensory systems makes its own unique contributions. Indeed, because each system functions specifically in relation to certain qualities, there is no way in which one sensory system can completely compensate for the absence of another. Even synesthesia depends upon the recall of the particular qualities that individual sensory systems make possible.

Although one's ability to use the sensory systems as avenues for experience is affected by maturation, the manner in which such abilities are used is affected by far more than maturation. What one is able to experience through any of the sensory systems depends, for example, not only on the characteristics of the qualities in the environment but also on the purposes, on the frames of reference, or on what Neisser refers to as the anticipatory schemata[12] that the individual has acquired during the course of his life. Perception, as Neisser puts it, is a cognitive event.[13] Just how factors such as prior learning and expectation affect one's perception of the world will be discussed later. The main point here is that the sentient human is not simply a passive material that, like moist clay, receives the impress of the empirical world, but is an active agent that selects and organizes aspects of that world for cognition.[14]

The reciprocity between what the organism does to the world and what the world does to the organism is dramatically illustrated by cross-cultural research on perception and by work on sensory deprivation. With respect to the latter, it has been found that the absence of light during the course of maturation can have irreversible effects on an organism's ability to see. Kittens between four and twelve weeks of age, whose eyes have been occluded, are unable to see when the occlusions are removed.[15] Lack of access to light during critical periods of development has a nonreversible impact on a kitten's sight. Even with the occlusions removed, the kitten remains blind. What this research suggests is that the firing of certain neurons requires an environmental trigger, the absence of which leaves them in a latent condition that, beyond a critical period, renders them inoperable. The concept of readiness here suggests that if an organism does not have opportunities to use certain capacities at critical periods in its life, it will not be able to use them once that period has passed.

This research was, of course, performed on kittens, but it is suggestive of questions having to do with the kinds of opportunities provided to children in school and in the culture at large. What kinds of stimuli do we fail to provide in schools, and, what abilities do we, therefore, neglect developing? What are the long-range consequences of such neglect? If one had a map of the mind that identified the varieties of cognitive capacity that human beings possessed, it might be possible to describe the qualities and tasks encountered in the environment in relation to those capacities. If one were then able to plot the incidence of their use within a culture—or a school—one would, in principle, be able to determine the magnitude of the opportunities the culture or the school provided for particular capacities to be developed. Perhaps we would find that each home and each subculture, as well as each culture, provide different opportunities for individuals to achieve particular forms of mental competence.[16]

Although the research described places great emphasis on the contributions of environmental conditions to stimulate or provide the organism with the opportunity to use certain capacities, the way in which an organism treats the qualities that make up the environment are not simply a function of the qualities as such. *Which* particular qualities the organism chooses to attend to and *how* he decides to respond are not completely influenced by the qualities themselves. A bridge, for example, can be perceived as a structure to serve as the theme for a poem, as a means for calculating height or length, or for estimating the amount of time it will take to cross at forty-seven miles per hour. Research on hemispheric specialization suggests that different brain functions will be utilized in dealing with each of these tasks.[17] It is likely, furthermore, that what an individual knows how to do and what he enjoys doing creates a response tendency that increases the probability that certain modes of thought will become characteristic. The painter will characteristically view the bridge as an expressive form having shape, scale, and color or as a candidate for a painting. The poet is likely to view the bridge as subject matter for a poem or epigram. The engineer regards it as an achievement in managing stress. Each construes the bridge in different terms, the terms with which each is most competent. As Ernst Gombrich once observed: "The painter does not paint what he can see, he sees what he is able to paint."

One can only speculate on the consequences of competency on the development of human capacity. Might it be that the development of certain competencies are achieved only at the cost of allowing others to atrophy?

What we have noted thus far is not only that there is a transactional or reciprocal relationship between the qualities of the environment and the cognitive structures or anticipatory schemata an organism possesses, but also that perception itself is constructive. This point has been mentioned earlier, but it is worth emphasizing particularly because the constructive character of perception has been underplayed in some psychological theories. Consider, for example, that in some psychological theories the qualities that constitute the environment are referred to as stimuli.[18] As a term, "stimuli" connotes that environmental conditions are the major, if not the sole, determinant of the response. What the concept of stimulus neglects is the fact that what constitues a stimulus, that is, what stimulates, is itself in part a function of how the qualities that make up the so-called stimulus are perceived. Like the term "input," which almost automatically suggests the term "output," the term "stimulus" almost automatically suggests "response," implying very little in the way of an intervening or mediating process. Such a theoretical view implies that the major focus of experimental attention should be upon the qualities of the stimulus rather than on the frames of reference the organism is likely to use to construe its qualities. When one is conducting experiments upon organisms much simpler than man, such a theoretical framework might have utility. With man, it can only lead to vastly oversimplified conceptions of the sources of human action.[19]

The move away from theories of mental structure as a way of understanding human activity was initially motivated by the desire to make psychological inquiry scientifically empirical; introspection was considered unreliable, and the "mind" was as too close to the metaphysics discussed in departments of philosophy. If psychology were to become scientifically respectable, neither introspection nor metaphysics would do.[20] Yet, what can a psychology be that neglects the mind? I am happy to report that some psychologists are returning to the study of mental life and, in the process, they are employing ingenious methods to describe and interpret how the mind functions. One of the most prolific and influential members of the group is Roger Shepard.[21]

In a wide-ranging, imaginative array of studies of mental imagery, Shepard has devised some ingenious methods of externalizing internal processes.[22] His work is indicative of the growing interest in mental life, and the creation of a new journal that focuses exclusively on imagery is perhaps an even stronger indication of interest in this area.[23]

Thus far, I have tried to identify some of the contributions the senses make to our awareness of the environment. I have also tried to illuminate the link between what is regarded as sense data and cognition. Because the senses have often been separated from the mind, their contributions to thinking have often been unappreciated. Activities that appear to rely upon the use of the senses or upon affect are often regarded as nonintellectual, that is, as activities that make little demand upon thinking or human intelligence. This tradition, one which is not only reflected in our psychological discourse but in our educational policies, is based upon a limited, and, I believe, educationally counterproductive view of mind. The formation of concepts depends upon the construction of images derived from the material the senses provide. Such concepts are developed from the qualities possessed by particulars from which general schemata are construed.

Language and Concept Formation

Why is it that knowing is related in a fundamental way to the experience that the senses make possible? Simply because experience always requires a content. One must be able to experience something in order to know it. Even the experience of nothingness depends upon our ability to imagine what it means. Because experience is a necessary condition for knowing, and because the character of experience is dependent upon the qualities to which it is directed, and because those qualities are picked up by our biological apparatus—the senses—to experience, and, hence, to know, one must interact with a content that one or more of the senses make possible. Because the kind of content the senses pick up is specific to their nature, the quality of experience will depend upon what one's senses have access to and upon how well one is able to use them.

Such a view of knowing and concept formation seems to leave little room for the function of language, something that some hold to be the sine qua non of both thinking and knowing. I want to argue that propositional language functions largely as a surrogate for experience with qualitative material.[24] We have a vocabulary that we use to refer to the qualities of the world, but this vocabulary is only a gross representation of the qualities themselves. In fact, we are able to differentiate thousands of qualities for which we have no vocabulary. The same is true for grammatical construction—sentences or phrases. We operate by using language as it is conventionally defined, and in doing so we get along quite well. But even here what phrases mean is dependent upon our ability to recall the referents of the terms and the relations that hold among them. Indeed, metaphors like "I'll pick you up tomorrow" are understood not because a person will actually be picked up but because picking up objects and giving a person a "lift" have much in common. In both cases the common attributes of the referents as experience (being "picked up" and giving someone "a lift") allow us to invent metaphors that relate quite comfortably to them. The metaphor is derived from the common characteristics of the experience.

Following Sir Herbert Read, I am arguing that the cultivation of the senses is a primary means for expanding our consciousness.[25] Learning how to represent what we have experienced is a primary means for contributing to the expanded consciousness of others. Thus, a culture or a school program that dulls the senses by neglect or disrespect thwarts human aptitude and undercuts the possibilities of the human mind.

This point is worth special emphasis because of the tradition that argues that concept formation is always dependent upon the use of discursive language. According to some, there can be no thinking without the use of discourse because it is not possible to form a concept that is not itself linguistic. Adam Schaff makes this point this way:

> When we adopt the monistic standpoint, we reject the claim that language and thinking can exist separately and independently of one

another. Of course, we are talking about specifically *human* thinking, in other words about *conceptual* thinking. Thus we assert that in the process of cognition and communication, thinking and using a language are inseparable elements of one and the same whole. Integration is so perfect and interdependence is so precise that neither element can ever occur independently, in a "pure" form. That is precisely why the functions of thinking and language may not be treated separately, let alone contrasted with one another.[26]

Such a view of thinking appears to me to be questionable on several counts. What, for example, does one do to explain the work of artists, composers, athletes, cooks, and others whose primary form of representation depends on the creation of qualitative relationships. Is it really the case, for example, that Bach had to conceptualize the Brandenberg Concertos in words before he was able to transform the words into music? Perhaps Bach's musical achievements were not a product of thinking at all? But, if this is the case, what were they due to? Inspiration? The muse, perhaps? Such explanations will hardly do. Even Noam Chomsky, for whom discursive language plays a central role in the operation of mind, recognizes that thinking exceeds the limits of discourse. He writes:

> Is it the case, for example, that humans necessarily think in language? Obvious counterexamples immediately come to mind. Our only evidence of any substance is introspective, the introspection surely tells me that when I think about a trip to Paris or a camping expedition to the Rockies, the few scraps of internal monologue that may be detected hardly convey, or even suggest the content of my thought. In struggling with a mathematical problem, one is often aware of the role of a physical, geometrical intuition that is hardly expressible in words, even with effort and attention . . .[27]

The point that Chomsky is making about the fact that language does not exhaust the activities we refer to as thinking is significant for several reasons. First, it challenges the widely held belief that thinking *requires* discursive or mathematical mediation. What Chomsky recognizes is that the forms of human thought are multiple and that language in its conventional sense is only one among many of the forms that it employs. Second, it suggests that thinking and experiencing cannot be easily separated. I believe that no form of experience is possible without cognitive activity and that such activity is itself what we mean by thinking. Even the awareness of sensation requires some modicum of thought for what else would make awareness possible? Once we recognize that perception is a cognitive event, the hard and fast distinctions between sensation, perception, and cognition begin to pale.[28] The behaviors that do not require one to think are those that are a function of the reflex response: the knee jerk, the eyewink, the dilation of the pupil in the eye. But *experiencing* the qualities of sound, of touch, of taste requires attention, selection, comparison, and judgment. It is very easy for someone to miss experiencing the qualities in his or her perceptual field. When we say that some people do not learn from their experience, it is because we ourselves fail to recognize that the experience we assume they are having, from which they might learn, they, in fact, are missing. Not to see the connection between an act and its consequences—something that frequently happens when one is trying to learn—is not to have a particular kind of experience, the experience represented by the recognition of the relationship.

An Expanded View of Knowledge

The reader will note that I am arguing that knowing depends upon experience, either the kind of experience that emanates from the sentient being's contact with the qualities of the environment or from the experiences born of the imagination. My use of the term "knowing" differs from the concept of "knowledge" as used by philosophers of either an analytic or a positivistic orientation. In more conventional usage, the term knowledge is restricted to being a "warranted assertion,"[29] of which there are two kinds: analytic and synthetic. Analytic assertions are propositions that are true by definition, such as those used in symbolic logic and in mathematics: $30 \times 20 = 600$ is an example of an analytic assertion or proposition. Such propositions are regarded as true or false if they are or are not consistent with certain axioms defined within the system. Here consistency, rather than empirical verification, is the means for determining the meaning and truthfulness of the proposition. We regard $2 + 2 = 4$ as true, not by examining the contents of the world but by understanding our agreement to use terms in a particular way.

Synthetic propositions are assertions about empirical conditions that can be falsified through specific operations that a community of competent inquirers can employ. What counts as knowledge are propositions about the world that are capable of falsification but which have not been falsified. Notice that in this conception of knowledge the role of the proposition is crucial. There can be no knowledge unless an assertion or claim about some empirical matter has been made, and assertions always require propositional form. But even more, the assertion must be capable in principle of being falsified by a set of operationally defined methods. Thus, the claim that there are fourteen cars on the parking lot can be verified by anyone who knows what cars are like, what parking lots are like, and how to count. If methods of verification cannot be employed or *in principle* imagined, the assertion is regarded simply as an utterance, something that is literally without meaning.

The reason this view of knowledge has been so attractive to so many is because, by regarding knowledge as propositional and by requiring publicly available tests of its validity, it was believed possible to rid philosophy of metaphysics and unverifiable utterance—sources of confusion and obscurantism. Both positivistic and linguistic analysis were a kind of philosophic hygiene that eliminated the dross from philosophic literature.

But note that for synthetic propositions the referents for the propositions are still nonpropositional matters; they are qualities that the sensory systems pick up. Cars and parking lots are sensory before they are linguistic. In this sense, talk about those qualities is not the same as experience itself. When they are described through discourse, a reduction occurs, particularly when the talk is propositional rather than literary or poetic. In some cases, the reduction is radical. Thus, a dilemma emerges. As one moves away from propositions and operational procedures as conditions necessary for falsification, the prospects for securing consensus about the validity of claims is diminished. Yet to restrict the term knowledge and, by implication, knowing to what propositions about qualities can reveal is to exclude from the arena of knowledge all that propositions as a form of representation cannot embody. That price, in my view, is far too high. Shakespeare's rendering of jealousy in Othello, Picasso's revelations of the horror of Guernica, Schiller's "Ode to Joy" cannot be reduced to propositions. The concern for validation and falsification has been so great that all else simply was regarded as suspect at best. For some, not even *that* level of cognitive status is attained since "suspect" implies that a nonlinguistic form of representation can, in principle, provide meaningful information about the world. Some would not regard anything as meaningful that cannot be refuted by "objective" operational procedures.

The educational and political ramifications of the views I have described are not simply the playthings of philosophers. They are far more than educational or philosophic exotica. Commitment to a particular view of knowledge has consequences not only for school curricula, but also for the conduct of research, for the funding of research, for promotion at universities, for the definition of professional competence, for access to publication in professional journals, and even, as I have suggested earlier, for shaping our conception of mind.[30]

In pointing out the limitations of the view of knowledge I have just described, I am not suggesting that propositions about the world have nothing to tell us or that their information load is necessarily small. I am saying, first, that propositions about empirical matters must relate to those matters through direct contact or through imagination to be meaningful and, second, that propositions as *one* form of representation cannot in principle contain all that can be known or experienced about the empirical world. Furthermore, the restriction of knowledge and, by implication, understanding to propositional discourse about the phenomenal world distorts our view of reality and has a wide array of ancillary political and educational consequences that are deleterious to the development of human ability and to human understanding. I am attempting in this book to argue the case for a more ecumenical view of the forms that make diverse kinds of understanding possible in the hope that, with such a view, a more generous conception of curriculum and evaluation can be forged. Methodological dogmatism, even in the name of truth, can fetter man's capacity to know.

The view that knowing must be embodied within propositions leads to the belief that certain modes of thought are affective or emotive, while others are cogntive and intelligent. Meaning is the product of the one, and expressiveness is the product of the other. The sciences become the avenue to truth, and the arts the roads to pleasure and emotional release. Understanding is the exclusive issue of verified propositions, and poetic statement is regarded as noncognitive.

I find this view of knowing and of thinking curious. One's experience of the world is basically qualitative. Concepts initiate in the forms of experience that the senses make possible. When they are rendered into discourse, a transformation takes place, and there is always a reduction in the process. The forms of conceptualization from one to the other are not the same. To hold that it is the discursive reduction that carries the meaning, and that the content that gives meaning to it is meaningless, is to put the cart before the horse. In the desire to tame and harness meaning so that it abides by conventional rules for purposes of verification, those forms of knowing that lie outside the realm in which such rules can be applied have been made "noncognitive."

Are There Nonqualitative Concepts?

But, one might legitimately ask, are all concepts at base qualitative? What about concepts that apparently are not tied directly to the qualities of the world, concepts such as "infinity," "category," "nation," "justice," "hope." We typically use such terms without needing to think of their referents. We communicate with an automaticity that does not take time for concrete exemplification. But this bypassing of the qualities to which the term refers should not be taken to mean that, because the term is a so-called "abstraction" (all terms are abstract), it is not rooted in sensory material. Suppose someone did not understand the meaning of the term "infinity" and wanted you to help him grasp its meaning. The task you would probably undertake would be to illustrate the meaning of the concept through material that was visual or visualizable. One attempts to make verbal labels meaningful by providing the label with a content that one can experience directly or can imagine, an image that gives the label meaning. Indeed, one might well ask whether it is possible to derive any meaning whatsoever from a label if the content to which that label refers cannot be conceptualized, that is, imagined.

It is interesting to observe that the significance of the role played by the senses in conception is revealed in the Latin root of the term "intuition." That root is *intuitus*, which means "to look upon."[31] To have intuition is to have insight, to see something that was once unseen, to grasp through the senses. Hence, once having an idea explained, a person might exclaim, "I see!" signifying a grasp of the image that gives the explanation meaning.

Because concept formation occurs within and among each of the sensory systems' contacts with the environment, the way that environment is known will be largely influenced by the particular sensory system or systems we use in dealing with it. The objects that populate the environment almost always possess qualities that can be experienced by using a variety of sensory systems. A rose is not just its aroma, but also its color and texture and the relationship of these qualities to each other. A person is not simply his visual appearance, but his voice, the distinctive character of his personal traits, the sound of his walk. Even perfume is known by more than its scent; the identification of the scent with the form of the bottle in which it is packaged is of crucial importance to perfume manufacturers as well as to those who buy perfume. Even Joy, reputedly the world's most expensive perfume, would not be likely to sell well, even at bargain prices, if it were packaged in a yogurt container. The fact that the qualities of the environment are multiple means that the ways in which these qualities can be known are also potentially multiple. The ability to experience the multiplicity of environmental qualities is one of the aims I believe educational programs should attempt to achieve.

Insofar as the qualities of the world are multiple and insofar as concept formation with respect to those qualities is multiple, it is unlikely that one's conception of complex qualitative wholes is likely to be singular. What, for example, does it mean to have a conception of autumn? For some, it is something that begins during the ninth month of the Julian calendar; for others, it is that period during the year when daylight diminishes and darkness expands. For teachers, I suppose, autumn means the appearance of thirty new faces and the beginning of a new school year. Autumn can also be the time in which the sharp chill of the early evening blends magically with the aroma of burning leaves. For those not tied to the restrictions of a dictionary, autumn is a multiplicity of meanings, each the offspring of how the season is experienced.

Summary and Significance

What, then, are the major points addressed thus far? First, that concept formation is itself biologically rooted in the sensory systems that humans possess. Our ability to experience different qualities constituting the environment through the information pickup systems represented by our senses provides the material out of which concepts are made. Thus, concepts are formed not only in visual, but in gustatory, olfactory, tactile, and auditory form. We have a conception of roundness not only because we know what a circle or a sphere looks like but because we know how it feels.

Second, that meaning is itself not only diverse in character but that the kinds of meanings we secure are affected by our purpose, the frame of reference we use, the degree of differentiation we have achieved. What we experience depends in part on what nets we cast. Third, for an idea to be meaningful—say, the idea of random mutation and natural selection—the organism must initially be able to imagine or recall the referents for the terms that collectively express the idea. Randomness, for example, is the specific qualitative characteristic of a process or the characteristics of the product of that process. When distributions do not possess the characteristics one expects from a process that purports to be random, we examine the process in order to check. In the end, it is the congruence between the term and the qualities that we experience that provides warrant for the label "random."

Similarly, a genetic mutation is recognized because it is qualitatively different from its genetic parents. Again, it is the qualities that constitute our conception of mutation that enable us to justify claims about a particular gene being a mutant. Even when an idea or concept has no empirical referent—subatomic particles, the *initial* conceptualization of

DNA as a double helix, and so forth—the concept or idea is conceivable as an imaginative construction. Seen in this way, inferences and hypotheses are derived for purposes of experimentation. Even in what is regarded as the most abstract of fields, mathematics, images are at work. Einstein described his own psychological processes in this regard:

> The words or the language, as they are written or spoken, do not seem to play any role in my mechanism of thought. The psychical entities which seem to serve as elements in thought are certain signs and more or less clear images which can be "voluntarily" reproduced or combined. . . . But taken from a psychological viewpoint, this combinatory play seems to be the essential feature in productive thought— before there is any connection with logical construction in words or other kinds of signs which can be communicated to others. The above-mentioned elements are, in my case, of visual and some of muscular type. Conventional words or other signs have to be sought for laboriously only in a secondary stage, when the mentioned associative play is sufficiently established and can be produced at will.[32]

The utilities of visualization in mathematical inquiry and scientific research appear to be straightforward. With visualization, complex relationships can be reflected upon in space rather than in time. With qualities arrayed in space, certain relationships can be examined, the load on memory reduced, and forms of conceptual manipulation are made possible that would be very cumbersome if a linear, temporal mode of thought needed to be employed. Indeed, the utilities of such thinking are evidenced in the use of holography and through computer displays that produce images that help researchers understand relationships that could not be grasped in any other way.[33]

A fourth point is that, while the kinds of concepts that are made possible through the several sensory systems can occur simultaneously, only one concept in the same sensory system can be experienced at the same time. For example, we are able to imagine a speech being given, hear the words being spoken, and see the setting in which it occurs. We are able to conceive of a melody and place the locale in which it takes place or which it expresses; program music is composed to generate such experience. But what we cannot do is to imagine two melodies simultaneously. We might shift our attention from one to the other, but we cannot experience both at once. Similarly, we cannot experience two visual images at once. We are able to imagine a complex visual array, one made up of a variety of visual elements, but we are unable to visualize red and yellow squares that occupy the same conceptual space in our imagination. The ability to employ different forms of conceptualization simultaneously has, of course, extremely important assets.

Being able to visualize, to hear, and to feel, through imagination, aspects of a situation or problem with which we have to cope provides us with opportunities for rehearsal. We can play out in our imaginative life what we would otherwise have to act upon in order to know. We can stop and think in a context where the imaginative checking out of alternatives is possible before those alternatives are pursued in the empirical world. The Gedanken experiment is, in the sciences, the paradigm case of such activity. Less sophisticated beginnings of such activity are to be found under more ordinary circumstances: the daydreaming of children and adults, the planning of summer holidays in winter, reflection on choices of furniture and clothing, the multitude of pensive activities that fill our waking hours. The fact that we are not restricted to one mode of conceptualization at a time allows us to secure a fuller picture of the conditions with which we must deal and makes it possible to treat them experientially as ideas before we take action.

Is the ability to engage in such thinking educable? Can we increase our skill in imaginative conceptualization through schooling? If we could, what might be the consequences of such newly developed skills? Would they contribute to the solution of problems that now appear unresolvable? To what extent, for example, does productive mathematical thinking depend upon one's ability to use skills such as visualization? Such questions are of central importance to the formation of curriculum policy. But before attempting to explore some answers, it is necessary to examine the other side of the conceptual coin, the manner in which concepts take public form and the contributions that they in turn make to cognition. For this, we turn to the process of representation.

Notes

1. Lawrence W. Downey, *The Task of Public Education*, Chicago: University of Chicago Press, 1960.

2. For a treatment of cognition as essentially dealing with thought mediated by language, see, for example, Barry F. Anderson, *Cognitive Psychology*, New York: Academic Press, 1975.

3. Palo Alto, California, schools report no set pattern for when art is taught, except for the family-elected, after-school art program. *Source*: Addison School, Creekside School.

4. Jean Piaget notes that "the affective and cognitive mechanism always remain indissociable although distinct..." See his *The Child and Reality*, New York: Grossman, 1973, p. 47.

5. John Dewey, *Art As Experience*, New York: G. P. Putnam's Sons, 1958, p. 46.

6. Rudolf Arnheim notes that in early Greek philosophy, "Sensory perception and reasoning were established as antagonists, in need of each other but different from each other in principle. . . . The mistrust of ordinary perception marks Plato's philosophy profoundly." See his *Visual Thinking*, Berkeley: University of California Press, 1969, pp. 6, 8.

7. Plato, *The Republic*, tr. with introd. by Francis MacDonald Cornford. New York: Oxford University Press, 1951.

8. See Karl Popper, *The Open Society and Its Enemies*, London: Routledge and Kegan Paul, 1945.

9. In 1977 the following were the top five states in terms of funds expended for gifted and talented students:

State	State funds	Number of students served
California	$15.4 million	190,000
Pennsylvania	13.0 million	29,000
Florida	12.0 million	20,000
North Carolina	8.0 million	39,000
Georgia	4.3 million	26,000

Source: Dorothy Sisk, "Education of the Gifted and Talented: A National Perspective," *Special Education Yearbook*, 1979.

10. Ulric Neisser, *Cognition and Reality: Principles and Implications of Cognitive Psychology*, San Francisco: W. H. Freeman, 1976.

11. According to Burton L. White, the newborn will "exhibit a rudimentary capacity for visual motor pursuit. By six weeks, flexible visual focusing begins and ability is fully developed by four months . . ." See his *Human Infants: Experience and Psychological Development*, Englewood Cliffs, N.J.: Prentice-Hall, 1971.

12. Neisser, *Cognition and Reality*.

13. *Ibid*.

14. See John Dewey, *Experience and Education*, New York: Macmillan, 1938; Jean Piaget, *The Development of Thought: Equilibration of Cognitive Structures*, New York: Viking Press, 1977.

15. Stephen W. Kuffler and John G. Nicolls, *From Neuron to Brain: A Cellular Approach to the Function of the Neuron Systems*, Sunderland, Mass.: Sinovar Associates, 1976, esp. chap. 19.

16. Michael Cole, *Culture and Thought: A Psychological Introduction*, New York: Wiley, 1974.

17. Michael S. Gazzaniga and Roger W. Sperry, "Language after Section of the Cerebral Commissures," *Brain*, 90: 131–248, No. 1, 1967.

18. In behaviorism the term has a central place, i.e., stimulus-response. This pair of terms was at the core of the theory developed by one of America's most influential educational psychologists. E. L. Thorndike.

19. Indeed, it is important to distinguish between behavior and action. For an excellent commentary on this distinction, see Thomas Green, "Teaching, Acting, and Behaving," *Harvard Educational Review*, 34:507–524, Fall 1964.

20. J. B. Watson, in *Behavior: An Introduction to Comparative Psychology*, New York: Henry Holt, 1914, p. 8, argued against introspection in psychology in 1914. He wrote: "One must believe that two hundred years from now, unless the introspection method is discarded, psychology will still be divided on the question as to whether auditory sensations have the quality of 'extension,' whether intensity is an attribute which can be applied to color, whether there is a difference in 'texture' between image and sensation; and upon many hundreds of others of like character . . . The time seems to have come when psychology must discard all reference to consciousness. . . ."

21. Roger Shepard, "Cognitive Processes That Resemble Perceptual Processes," in *Handbook of Learning and Cognitive Processes*, ed W. N. Estes, Hillsdale, N. J.: Erlbaum Associates, 1978.

22. See, especially, Roger Shepard, "Form, Formation and Transformation of Internal Representations," in *Information Processing and Cognition: The Loyola Symposium*, ed. R. Salso, Hillsdale, N. J.: Erlbaum Associates, pp. 87–122.

23. *Journal of Mental Imagery*, begun in 1977.

24. Arnheim, *Visual Thinking*.

25. Herbert Read writes on the contribution of art to consciousness: "What is now suggested, in opposition to the whole of the logico-rationalistic tradition, is that there exists a concrete visual mode of 'thinking,' a mental process which reaches its highest efficiency in the work of art. It is a mode of thinking which sustains that primary unity of perception and feeling found in the eidetic disposition. This primary unity develops into the unity of sensibility and reason

(sensation and ideas) and is then the basis of all imaginative and practical activity." See his *Education through Art*, New York: Pantheon, 1945.

26. Adam Schaff, *Language and Cognition*, ed. Robert S. Cohen, New York: McGraw-Hill, 1973, p. 118.

27. Noam Chomsky, "Foreword," in Schaff, *Language and Cognition*, ed. Cohen.

28. Neisser, *Cognition and Reality*.

29. A. J. Ayer, *Language, Truth, and Logic*, New York: Dover, n.d.

30. The style and content of professional journals perform an extremely important socializing function in a field of study since access to journals affects the young scholar's view of what is competent and influences his or her chances for publication and promotion.

31. The Latin root of intuition is *intuitus*, the noun of action from *intueri*, meaning to look upon, consider, contemplate. *Oxford English Dictionary*, Oxford, Eng.: Clarendon Press, 1961.

32. Gerald Holton, "Influences on Einstein's Early Work in Relativity Theory," *American Scholar*, 37: 959–979, Winter 1967–68.

33. For the educational utility of graphic aids, see, for example, J. C. Birkimer and J. H. Brown. "Graphical Judgmental Aid Which Summarizes Obtained and Chance Reliability Data and Helps Assess the Believability of Experimental Effects," *Journal of Applied Behavioral Analysis*, 12:523–533, Winter 1979. See also M. Effing, "Representing Image Formation in Lenses and Mirrors," *Physics Teacher*, 15:178–179, March 1977; M. P. Barrich, "Log-Log Plotting as a Tool in High School Physics," *Physics Teacher*, 10:37–39, January 1972; N. A. Feshbach *et al.*, "Demonstration of the Use of Graphics in Teaching Children Nutrition," *Journal of Nutrition Education*, 10:124–126, July-September 1978. For a discussion of the special capacities of holography, see T. Ouosh, *Three-Dimensional Imaging Techniques*, New York: Academic Press, 1976.

3

Forms of Representation

Some of the ways in which the sensory systems contribute to the formation of concepts were discussed in the previous chapter. But concepts, regardless of the form they take, are personal aspects of human experience, and, although they might provide illumination for those who have them, they are private and cannot be shared until they are made public. It is only when those experiences serve as the content for human expression that communication is possible and that the content of the experience is made social.

In order to achieve a social dimension in human experience, a means must be found to carry what is private forward into the public realm. This is achieved by employing what in this book is called *forms of representation*. Forms of representation are the devices that humans use to make public conceptions that are privately held. They are the vehicles through which concepts that are visual, auditory, kinesthetic, olfactory, gustatory, and tactile are given public status. This public status might take the form of words, pictures, music, mathematics, dance, and the like.

Consider the task of the painter. Imagine a painter taking a trip through a small midwestern town, say with a population of about 1,500. The town is located in Kansas, and the painter was born and raised in New York City. For him, the experience of the town is altogether special: the scale of the main street, the character of the storefronts, the pace and comportment of the people, the menus posted on the door of the diner, the slow-paced movement of the traffic in the streets, the expanse of sky that hangs cloudless overhead. There is, for him, a special kind of magic to the place; in certain respects it is a sort of throwback to a life that he occasionally glimpsed as a boy growing up in New York, but which has long since passed.

The qualities of his experience are multiple in form and meaning. They are visual, and they are dynamic. They are a mixture of images, sounds, textures, words, and the pervasive quiet brightness that seems to be everywhere. Upon reflection, he finds that his experience is punctuated at the beginning and at the end. It is bracketed in his imagination as a special event, "an object" to be recalled, an experience undergone in the spring of 1975. Intoxicated by it, he is moved to put on canvas and thus to stabilize what was fleeting yet vivid. To do this, he must use a form of representation, and, because he is a painter, he will use a visual image. He will try to create a set of visual relationships on a static surface that will adumbrate the character of that small Kansas town and his experience with it.

The options available to him are as numerous as the techniques at his command and his inventiveness in using them. What he is able to say about his experience in that town will be determined by a multiplicity of factors that comes into play as he puts brush to canvas: his concentration on certain aspects of the town, the technical skills at his disposal, the limits to which the paint will yield to his desires, and the extent to which he will yield to its demands. Ultimately, however, the task is one of representing his experience with a place. It is one of creating a publicly shareable image that will deliver to the competent eye an experience worth having.[1]

The decision to use paint as material and the visual image as medium for conveying his experience is, technically speaking, one of several options available. The town might have been rendered in dance, through drama, in poetry, or in prose. But for a painter the choice is obvious: an image made from paint and applied to a stretched canvas. For him, one might say, there is no choice. He does what he knows how to do. In fact, even his experience was shaped by his expressive skills, while, at the same time, the use of his expressive skills is guided by his experience.

Had our traveler been not a painter but a composer, the task would also have been one of image making,[2] but the form of representation would have been auditory rather than visual. The composer's task is to say about that town what can be said through music.

Suppose our traveler was neither a painter nor a composer, but a sociologist. Surely what is experienced would be influenced by what the sociologist knows how to do. It is likely that his conception of the town would be shaped by the sociological categories he knows. What the sociologist "asks for" will profoundly influence the nature of the answers he receives. Thus, whenever a form of representation is used (in this case sociological prose) there is a concomitant neglect of those qualities of the world which the form cannot "name." Neglect, in the case of our sociological traveler, should not be regarded as something unique to sociology. *Every* form of representation neglects some aspect of the world.[3] Just as perception itself must be selective in order to focus, so, too, must be the content that a form of representation can contain. Not everything can be said through anything. The selection of a form of representation is a selection of what can be used to transform a private experience into a public one. Forms of representation that will not take the impress of particular kinds of experience cannot, by definition, be used to convey them.

The selection of a form of representation not only functions as a vehicle for conveying what has been conceptualized, but forms of representation also help articulate conceptual forms. Consider an example from drawing. If one knows that one were going to draw, say, the diner in the town in Kansas, the character and the detail of the diner are likely to be looked for, seen, and remembered in a way that is much more intense, detailed, and vivid than if one were going to compose a piece of music about it or to describe it through the prose of sociology. The demands of the task guide one's perception. What one cannot see or imagine, one cannot draw.

Thus, it is possible to identify the several ways in which the selection of a form of representation influences not only the content of representation but the content of conception as well. First, as one becomes skilled in the use of particular forms of representation, the tendency to want to use such forms increases, and the focus that they engender is likely to become a salient frame of reference for perception.[4] The kinds of nets we know how to weave determine the kinds of nets we cast. These nets, in turn, determine the kinds of fish we catch. Second, the skills we possess in the use of particular forms of representation influence the extent to which what we know conceptually can be represented publicly. Someone who cannot sing might be able to compose great melodies, but they are not likely to be represented by him through song. The degree to which skills are absent or technique is weak is the degree to which the forms of representation are themselves weakened. Indeed, skill is regarded so highly by Olson that he considers intelligence itself to be "skill in a medium."[5] Third, the particular form of representation one selects places constraints upon what one is able to say, regardless of the level of skill one possesses or the variety of techniques one knows how to use. Some aspects of human experience are simply better expressed through some forms than through others. If it were possible to convey everything that humans wanted to convey with one or two forms of representation, the others would be redundant.

Consider, for example, the experience of suspense and how it might be portrayed through two different forms of representation, music and visual art. It is not difficult to imagine how that quality of experience we call suspense might be represented in music. As a matter of fact, it is likely that most readers can readily imagine the kind of music they might compose, even as they read these words. The image of the chase in old cowboy movies or the scores of old "who-dun-it" films come readily to mind. Because suspense is largely a temporal experience, music, which is also temporal, is an appropriate vehicle for representing it.[6]

But now try to imagine how suspense might be represented through a visual image. Here the task becomes considerably more difficult. Aside from some trite illustrations, it is very difficult to even conceive of, let alone paint or sculpt, a visual representation of such an experience. Visual images are more spatial than temporal; suspense is more temporal than spatial. The two are difficult to reconcile. The examples that one could provide are numerous, but the point remains the same. *The choice of a form of representation is a choice in the way the world will be conceived, as well as choice in the way it will be publicly represented.*

Perhaps one last example is in order. Assume that, for some reason, the only form of representation we were allowed to use was mathematics. Suppose, further, that during that period we thought of something quite humorous that we wanted to share with others. How might we use mathematics to express humor? How could we quip or be funny through addition or subtraction, calculus, geometry or algebra? To suggest that mathematics is difficult to use for representing humor is not to imply that it is not extremely useful for other things. Mathematics, like every other form of representation, is an appropriate vehicle for expressing some aspects of human consciousness, but not all aspects. To be restricted to it alone would eventually not only limit expression, but put the brakes on conception as well

Thus far, I have spoken of the use of forms of representation as though the direction of the activity was from conception to expression, from what is conceived to its transformation through a form of representation into a public image. While the process often does move in this direction, by no means is this the only way in which it can proceed. No one working with a material, whether words or other qualities, conceptualizes every detail prior to action. The process of working with material is, among other things, a heuristic process. Through it ideas are formed, negotiated, revised, discovered.[7] The course of inquiry seldom follows the path of an arrow. Indeed, some artists intentionally work in a way that fosters the adventitious, almost intuitively exemplifying the truth of Aristotle's observation that "art loves a chance."[8] Rather than trying to impose a preconceived image upon a material, their aim is to act and, from the action, to leave tracks, as it were, of where they have been. One such group was the abstract expressionists of whom the noted art critic Harold Rosenberg wrote:

> At a certain moment the canvas began to appear to one American painter after another as an arena in which to act – rather than a space in which to reproduce, redesign, analyze or "express" an object, actual or imagined. What was to go on the canvas was not a picture but an event.
>
> The painter no longer approached his easel with an image in his mind; he went up to it with material in front of him. The image would be the result of this encounter.[9]

For many artists the process is a matter of qualitative negotiation. Although the work might have been initiated as a desire to impose a concept upon pliable material, the work itself gradually begins to "participate" in the negotiations. Gradually the work "tells" the artist what is needed. What may have been begun as a lecture becomes a conversation. What may have been started as a monologue becomes a dialogue.

It should not be surprising that the process itself yields ideas that were not a part of the initiating conception. Working within forms of representation provides the individual with an opportunity not only to perform in the role of maker but in the role of critic as well. The actions one takes and the ideas one expresses are stabilized in the medium in which one works: one hears the music one plays, one reads the words one writes, one sees the images one creates.[10] Each of these stabilized public forms provides a content for analysis, revision, and appreciation. The first critic of an individual's efforts is the maker himself.

Perhaps nowhere is the critical function more obvious—though it exists in equal degree in other forms of representation—than it is in writing. The first drafts tht one produces are almost always riddled with ambiguities, uncertainties, lapses of logic, inconsistencies, errors in grammar, and the like. The creation of prose allows the editing process to proceed, to detect errors of omission and commission. In short, the written form makes it possible to refine thinking and to clarify meaning.

The opportunity to use a form of representation can generate ideas in at least two ways. First, the opportunity to act upon a material itself motivates one to think. Countless ideas are developed because of a need to present a paper at a professional meeting or to meet a deadline set by others. The demands of the occasion motivate the creation.

Second, as already indicated, the work to be produced is never wholly conceived prior to action. The process of working with a form of representation clarifies, confers detail, provides material upon which ideas can be worked out and corrections made.

Because different forms of representation emphasize the use of different sensory systems, the kinds of psychological processes they evoke are also likely to differ. We might well ask what this means for the development of cognition. If the kinds of mental skills or forms of intelligence one possesses are influenced by opportunities to use them, does it not seem likely that the forms of representation children have access to or are encouraged to use will shape the mental skills or forms of intelligence they will be able to develop?[11] If, furthermore, the kinds of meaning that individuals secure are related to the kinds of concepts they form and if different forms of representation tend to stimulate the formulation of different concepts, what does unequal emphasis on forms of representation mean for what people will come to know? When Basil Bernstein writes that the curriculum is a device not only for conveying the past but also a device for shaping consciousness, this is, I believe, what he had in mind.[12] When we define the curriculum, we are also defining the opportunities the young will have to experience different forms of consciousness. To have a musical consciousness, one must interact with music. To have a visual artistic consciousness, one must interact with visual art. To experience the poetics of language, poetry must be available. But the argument goes even further.

Man appears to have a *need* to shift the forms of consciousness he experiences. Even under the most difficult circumstances, when people lived at the edge of survival, they decorated their pots, inscribed their utensils, danced and created images that allowed their experience to vary. To know a set of conditions other than what they had known, images other than those they had typically encountered were created, often ingeniously. In this respect, one might regard forms of representation as mind-altering devices, as man-made vehicles through which the quality of experience is changed.

This view seems to me to be consistent with the way in which we lead our lives. We go to films, plays, and concerts, read history, and visit galleries and museums to have experiences that only such activities are likely to make possible. The experience, when it is successful, is mind altering. We come away refreshed, feeling better, sometimes even nourished by our break from routine and the forms of consciousness that dominate it. In this sense, variety contributes to our mental health.

Thus far, I have provided only a general definition of forms of representation. Perhaps it is time to be more specific.

A Visual Model

The phrase "form of representation" has been conceptualized to refer to the expressive medium used to make a conception public. Any form of representation one elects to use must convey information through its appeal to one or more of the sensory systems. Hence, a form of representation may be visual, auditory, tactile, kinesthetic, gustatory or olfactory. It is obvious that, in film, for example, forms of representation used are not only visual but auditory. It is obvious, also, that, in dance, forms of representation are not only visual and auditory but also kinesthetic. Speech conveys not only by "pointing to" referents that are visual, but also by its melody and cadence—auditory qualities that are central aspects of the message. Thus, forms of representation often combine and interact in the way in which they carry information forward.

In deciding to conceptualize "forms of representation" in terms of its expressive medium, other alternatives were considered and rejected. Music or the visual arts, for example, could have been identified as forms of representation. Yet, to conceptualize the term at this level of abstraction is to construct a virtually endless list of categories. I prefer, therefore, to regard the nature of the vehicle as a form of representation, rather than particular culturally defined means such as painting, music, dance, poetry, film. This means, of course, that in many of these vehicles several forms of representation will be used.

I also considered regarding a discipline such as philosophy, biology, history, sociology, or psychology as a form of representation. This, too, was rejected. The reason is that, although different disciplines use different terms and methods, all the social sciences, for example, are couched in propositional language, and, from that standpoint, the expressive medium they use to represent conceptions does not differ. Thus, overall, it appeared to me much more conceptually neat to define "form of representation" in relation to the nature of the expressive medium and thus to underscore the fact that the kinds of meanings we are able to secure depend in large measure on the varieties of sensory information we can experience. Forms of representation are a major source of such experience.

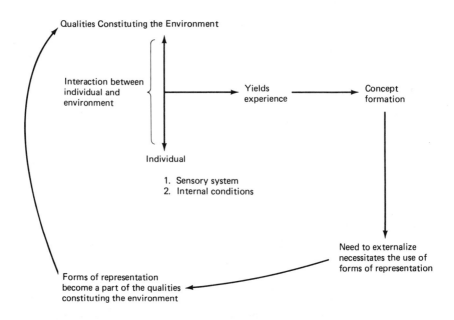

Figure 1. Model of Transactions between the Individual and the Environment.

Figure 1 presents schematically the relationships that hold between the various elements described thus far. At the center of the figure is a sentient individual possessing a sensory system, a personal history of prior learning, a set of attitudes or dispositions to focus in particular ways, and a set of representational skills. The individual interacts with an environment in which a variety of qualities are present. Out of this interaction, depending upon the individual's attitudes, purposes, and prior learning, aspects of that environment are construed and concepts formed. These concepts are formed out of the experience that the sensory systems make possible. They may subsequently be labeled through the use of discourse, although much of our experience will not take the impress of a verbal label. The kind of meaning the individual is likely to secure as he interacts with the qualities of the environment will depend upon the kinds of concepts he has formed, that is, it will depend upon the character of the qualities he has selected and experienced.

If the individual wishes to express the meanings secured from his interactions with those qualities, he must use some form of representation to do so. The particular form of representation chosen will be influenced by his skills as well as his purposes. Once he makes the transformation from the conception to the representation, the qualities he creates in these represented forms become a part of the environment upon which he can reflect further. The creation of new environmental qualities through the creation of a form of representation makes the editing process possible, which, in turn, makes it possible to revise, correct, and alter the ideas expressed through the form chosen. Thus, the creation of a form of representation serves not only as a means for conveying to others conceptions held by an individual; it also provides feedback for the individual.

Because the kind of experience an individual has depends upon the kinds of qualities the sensory systems pick up and because meaning depends upon experience, the character and distribution of qualities in an environment and the particular focus an individual brings to that environment affect the kind of meaning he is likely to have. Because particular forms of representaton often tend to emphasize particular qualities and utilize particular sensory systems, the kind of meaning that a single form of representation can express is limited. When the skills necessary for using a form of representation are not available or the encouragement to use them provided, the kinds of meanings that an individual might secure from such forms are likely to be forgone. For example, children who are given no opportunity to compose music are unlikely to secure the meanings that the making of music makes possible. Nor are they likely to regard the world in a way relevant to the creation of a musical equivalent.

It is important to reemphasize that the relationship between the individual and the environment is an interactive one. By this I mean that both the qualities of the environment *and* the individual's internal conditions affect the kind of experience or kinds of concepts that will be created. It is simply not the case that the qualities themselves determine what will be selected; nor is it the case that the individual will entirely project his internal conditions on the environment. There is a give-and-take in the process. Each factor makes its own contribution, and out of the interaction experience is born. This point is particularly germane for designers of curriculum.

Teachers and curriculum designers have no direct access to the internal conditions of the individual except through the qualities they create in the environment. Owners of expensive restaurants, people in the advertising industry, costume designers, and the like have long known of the importance of the environmental image. Although experience cannot be controlled or determined, it can be influenced by the conditions with which an individual interacts. What is true of the advertising industry is also true of the schools. The difference resides within their respective aims. The advertiser's aim is to manipulate the individual's behavior so that it affords a profit to the advertiser's client. Prediction of performance is a virtue; critical choice is a vice. In education, critical choice is a virtue; merely the successful manipulation of student behavior is a vice. What we seek in education is the cultivation of intelligence in the several modes in which it can operate. We seek to liberate rather than to control.

Modes of Treating Forms of Representation

The conceptualization of forms of representation as vehicles through which conceptions are externalized does not, by itself, describe the particular ways in which such forms can be treated so that some form of equivalent to a referent is created. Given any form of representation, say one that is visual or linguistic, how might it be treated so that it represents what someone is attempting to convey? To describe these ways of creating equivalents, the term *modes of treatment* has been formulated. Any form of representation can be treated in one or more of three modes: mimetic, expressive, and conventional.

The *mimetic mode* conveys through imitation, that is, it represents by replicating within the limits of the medium employed the surface features of some aspect of the qualitative world. There are, throughout human history, numerous examples of how mimetic modes of treatment function, from the use of hieroglyphics and pictographs that were employed to imitate the basic structural features of the visual world to the most advanced forms of photography and holography. Just what is it that mimetic modes of treatment do? Simply stated, they extract the salient features of some aspect of the world and re-present them as an image within some medium. They reproduce, to use Rudolf Arnheim's phrase, the structural equivalent of the features of world as experienced.[13]

The images of animals drawn on the walls of the Lescaux caves were probably the result of early man's interest in representing his observations of the world. It seems reasonable to assume that members of his community knew what they were intended to describe through their visual correspondence to their referents. In the use of hieroglyphics we have not only the abstracted visual representation of human figures, animals, furniture, and so forth, but we have them in a time sequence, a visual narrative that individuals are able to read. Hieroglyphics exemplify man's ability to combine both his spatial experience (the visual image) and his temporal experience by sequencing visual images in a form that not only parallels his visual experience at a particular point in time, but over time as well.[14]

If we look at a more modern example of the ways in which mimetic modes of treatment occur, it is vividly apparent in the use of highway signs. Particularly in Europe one will find signs that tell the driver what she or he can expect to encounter as the car moves down the highway: a curve in the road, a dip, animals crossing, zigzags, castles nearby, turn offs, and so forth. In each case, the image created shares some structural similarity with the object or situation it is designed to represent. Even though the form of representation is highly schematized, it presents the driver with as much information as he or she needs—and probably as much as can be handled at seventy miles per hour.

Consider also paintings and photographs. Suppose you wanted to know what the south of France looked like, or Chartres Cathedral, or your long-lost cousin Beatrice. You could, of course, read descriptions of such places and people and perhaps, if the writer were very skilled, it might be possible to gain a fairly good idea of their features. But a photograph or a painting will usually do the job much better. The special features of these places and people are more likely to be represented in a form that displays their characteristics through a medium and form of representation that is, itself, spatial than through one that is not. If we are trying to find someone disembarking from an airplane whom we have never met before, we would probably do better if we had a photograph than if we had a verbal description or a set of numbers describing the person's height and weight.

Perhaps the most telling example of the mimetic mode of treating visual forms of representation is to be found in the use of fingerprints. Here what one has is a direct visual imprint of a textured surface. The prints duplicate in virtually every detail the configurations of the surface of the fingers. Indeed, the correspondence is so close that among several million examples of prints on file in the FBI offices in Washington, no two are identical. One print is structurally isomorphic with the finger of a particular individual.

Given the utility of mimesis, it is curious to me to encounter Nelson Goodman's assertion that "A Constable painting of Marlboro Castle is more like any other picture than it is like the castle. . . ." or that "None of the automobiles off an assembly line is a picture of the rest."[15] I find these statements curious because we do, in fact, expect a portrait to represent, that is to say, to look like the sitter. If it does not, we are disappointed. And if we go into an automobile showroom, select a car and ask the salesman to order the same car, except in a different color, we are in fact using the car on the showroom floor as a model that we expect our car, when delivered, to duplicate. If we find that another model has arrived instead, or that the grill has been altered, or that another motor has been installed, or that different tires have been affixed, we not only have cause for complaint, but for canceling our order as well. A painting of Malborough Castle looks more like any other painting than the castle itself *only* if we choose to disregard its image and pay attention to the paint, canvas, stretcher, and frame.

Or consider still another example, the use of a prototype in the production of automobiles. It is standard practice to build prototype automobiles that in every respect are to be reproduced on the assembly line. Cars coming off the line duplicate these prototypes, which themselves are representations of designers' and engineers' conceptions. When a car coming off the line does not possess the features of the prototype, there is (or should be) a callback: something has gone amiss.

What such practices exemplify are efforts at mimesis, the prototypical model being the standard against which other cars coming off the line are to be appraised. In this way, as well as through the pictures and specifications provided in sales brochures, a mimetic function is performed. Like the highway signs, the prototype describes what is to be found when the journey is completed. It "pictures" in detail, ideally as a perfect replica, what workers, buyers, and management are to find when the work has been completed. In this sense, one car does indeed stand for another.

Now it is true that in some respects a painting of a car is more like any other painting or car than it is like a person or like some other thing. But that is true only if we shift context and disregard the function of representation. A scientific formula—H_2O—is more like any other formula—CO_2—than it is like water. We can always, I suppose, choose to disregard the intended function of a form in order to attend to another, and for some purposes such disregard might be functional. But Goodman's argument that imitation is largely irrelevant to representation is, I believe, unsound. Man has for thousands of years represented through mimesis. Indeed, techniques such as perspective were invented to make more credible the representations attempted.[16] This is not to say that paintings or even photographs are simply copies in the same way that fingerprints or death masks are copies. Idiosyncratic expression and interpretation are always present, at least to some degree. It is to say that we have learned how to read schematized images and that, for a great many kinds of information, we do not require the degree of mimesis that fingerprints provide.

Most of the examples I have used thus far are visual, but mimesis occurs in other forms of representation as well. Auditory forms of representation, such as music, can be composed to imitate the sound of thunder, running brooks, riders on horseback, and so forth. Words can be onomatopoeic. Tactile forms can be created to imitate a wide range of other tactile qualities, and so forth. The point here is that the imitation of selected features of the phenomenal world through an empirically available material has been and is one of the major means through which representation is achieved.

There is another point about the mimetic mode of treatment that is so obvious that it is often neglected. That is, for the purposes of mimesis, the closer the form of representation is to the content represented, the closer the mimesis is likely to be. Thus, to represent what is visual, forms of representation that provide visual information are, in general, likely to be more revealing than forms that provide other kinds of information. To know how something sounds, forms of representation that emphasize the auditory are more appropriate than forms that emphasize the visual. To know what someone said, a duplication of the words is more appropriate than a picture. This is not to suggest that transformations of experience from one sense modality to representation in forms that emphasize another should not or do not occur. Such a suggestion would mean the demise of literature. It is to suggest that mimetic functions tend to operate most successfully when the sense modality emphasized in the form of representation is like that which it aims to represent.

Allow me one further observation. In many situations the meaning of an experience is not simply the function of the experience secured through one of the senses, but, rather, of the interaction among the "data" picked up by the several senses. Consider discourse. When people talk, the meanings conveyed do not simply rely on what is said but on how it is said as well. The intonation and emphasis people give to the words they use, the gestures they make while speaking, their expression, the context in which what they have to say is said, what preceded in the conversation, and so forth. The absence of such features in transcripts of discourse can radically alter the meanings that, in fact, were conveyed when the discourse occurred.[17] To pick the varieties of information that accompany the discourse itself—if, indeed, one can talk about the "discourse itself" since it is never by itself—a variety of sensory systems must operate, and one must know how to read the meanings that the content they make possible provides. The ability to reconstruct varieties of information through sound and sight, tempo and context, is one of the virtues of film. Perhaps that is one of the reasons why film is so captivating and compelling. The absence of such contextual information in so much research on teaching might be one of the reasons why, on the whole, it has been so uninformative. More information is left out of most research reports on teaching than is included within them.

A second kind of treatment used to shape forms of representation is the *expressive mode*. By expressive, I mean that what is represented is not the surface features of the object or event, but, rather, its deep structure or, in other words, its expressive character. Consider the movement of a jet airplane speeding down a runway about to take off. The plane moves along very slowly and gradually increases its speed. Its speed continues to increase and about three-quarters of the way down the runway its nose rises and, like a duck leaving a lake, it lifts off the surface of the earth. Such an experience, if we were standing on the observation deck of an airport building, would be auditory as well as visual. We would experience a stark white form accelerating and gradually becoming nothing more than a small dark speck against the vast expansive blue sky. It is this movement, this gentle, graceful takeoff, the sound of the jet engines gradually diminishing in volume, the plane shrinking in size as it moves into the sky that a dancer or a graphic artist might create. Such creations have little to do with the imitation of surface features, but much more to do with the experiences of acceleration and of a slow rise into the atmosphere. How these expressive qualities might be represented is precisely what the artist must create. There are no codified formulas for producing them. What the artist wants to do is not to imitate the surface features of a moving plane, but to reveal its essential properties, that is to say, its expressive character. Here, too, a kind of imitation is at work, but it is not imitation of things seen. Rather, it is an imitation of things felt. The form of representation is treated expressively rather than mimetically. The analogic relationship is not established through the imitation of appearance, but through the creation of a form that generates the expressiveness of slowly accelerating movement.

Why have artists been interested in such tasks? Why should such efforts occupy such a central place in the history of the arts? At least a part of the reason is because much of what is most important in human experience is not what is apparent, but, instead, what is felt about what is apparent. Things are not always what they appear to be on the surface. They need to be seen in terms of the kind of emotional life that they generate. The sense of curiosity displayed by a very young child exploring a new toy or the fear of an old man anticipating imminent death are not simply physical movements. Such configurations possess a pervasive quality that conveys to the sensitive perceiver the character of curiosity and fear. Expressive forms must penetrate the surface features. Just how such forms, whether human or not, can convey such qualities of life is not altogether clear. Gestalt and associationist theories of meaning hold competing views, but it is not necessary to explain these theoretical views here. What is important is to recognize that the expressive treatment of forms of representation does occur and does function to shape our experience.

If to know about the character of life in a school or classroom or a suburb or ghetto requires one to know not only about surface appearance but also about the character of life within, then it is imperative that those who wish to make such knowledge public use means that can convey the qualities they seek to express. It is here that expressive modes of treatment are crucial. In literature and in poetry artistic achievement is realized in the expressive character of the forms created, not because such forms are necessarily beautiful or pleasant but because, without them, the very content that the artist wishes to convey could not be expressed. The expressive mode of treatment is, therefore, not simply a pleasant affectation, a dressing up of content to make it more palatable; it is, itself, part and parcel of the content of the form of representation. When descriptions of emotionally loaded situations lack the emotionality that they hold for those who live in those situations, a significant kind of bias and distortion results. To use a form to represent life in the concentration camps at Buchenwald or Dachau that omits the character of life as experienced by the inmates is to render less than a partial view of those camps; it is to mislead.

A third type of treatment is the *conventional mode*. By conventional, I simply mean that, as individuals are socialized within a culture, they learn that certain conventions stand in the place of something else. A red light, a cross, the word "table," the flag, the almost wholly arbitrary vocabulary of our discursive language are examples of the conventional mode of treating forms of representation. Words and colors are neither mimetic (although at one time they might have been) nor expressive (although they might be used expressively as words are used in literature and in poetry). The relationship between the form and referent is arbitrary. "Pain" in English means something like a sharp, uncomfortable feeling, while in French it means bread. There is nothing in the word per se to commend it to one rather than to the other referent. What matters is that, within each culture, there is agreement among those who use the word concerning the referent. This is not to suggest that meanings, even those related to convention, lack variability in interpretation by different individuals. The range of the variance is far narrower, however, than it is in either of the other two modes of treatment.

There is, of course, an important and interesting difference between the mimetic and the expressive modes of treatment and the conventional mode. In both the mimetic and the expressive modes, analogic relationships operate. In each case what is created parallels some aspect of the form being represented. In the conventional mode of treatment, this is not the case. A table does not look like how it sounds. For a word or a sentence to have meaning, the individual must be able to imagine the referent for the term or terms employed. This does not mean that, for every word used, there is a corresponding image. We have so mastered discourse that we do not need to conjure up an image in order to speak or write. If we encounter a word whose referent we cannot imagine, however, we can have no conception of what it means. It is in this sense that language functions as a surrogate for an image. If the surrogate is to have meaning, we must be able to conceive of its referent, even when the referent is a so-called abstract category. This is why, when children do not understand a word, we try to help them by providing examples.[18]

The distinctions I have made between the mimetic, the expressive, and the conventional should not be taken to mean that a form of representation uses only one mode of treatment. The three are often combined. For example, much visual art, particularly painting, uses mimetic, expressive, and conventional elements within the same work. Literature and poetry exemplify the mimetic mode in the way in which the sounds of events are emulated, the expressive mode in the way in which the structure of the prose penetrates the surface features of the events portrayed, and the conventional mode through the standardized use of language and symbol.

But perhaps the most vivid example of a vehicle that combines varieties of representation and modes of treatment is to be found in film. The modern film not only lets us see how something looks or sounds, but, when artistically successful, it also enables us to experience the underlying structure of the event and places portrayed. Films such as *Breaking Away* give us not only a glimpse of a particular aspect of middle America—its streets, people, and the plant in which Indiana limestone is cut—it also makes it possible for us to participate vicariously in the race between the "Cutters" and the campus cycle team. Furthermore, the conventional and unconventional uses of language serve as vehicles through which we understand the interaction among the characters. Indeed, it is the "Italianization" of the English language from which so much of the film's comic quality emerges. In addition, the use of camera angle, the character of the film's music, and the skillful editing all combine to convey through all three modes of treatment the meanings that constitute the film itself. We not only acquire some sense of what Bloomington, Indiana, looks like, but we also get some sense of the tension between "town" and "gown." We not only encounter five adolescent males discussing their ambitions and fantasies, but we are helped to identify with them and to experience their triumphs and defeats. Film is an extremely potent vehicle through which forms of representation and modes of treatment can interact. It is the awareness of this potential that directors, writers, and actors exploit to inform us about the events and the people that they portray.

The Syntaxes of Forms of Representation

Thus far I have spoken of forms of representation and modes of treatment. The former are those vehicles human beings have invented to make public privately experienced conceptions. The latter are the means used to shape the forms used to express a conception. Thus auditory forms of representation such as music can be treated mimetically as in the musical imitation of a man on horseback, expressively as in romantic music, or conventionally as in music that has specifically been assigned conventional meaning, "God Save the Queen," for example. The way forms of representation are treated does not, however, reveal much about the manner in which the components within a form of representation are related. It is to that topic that we now turn.

All forms of representation are forms arranged. I refer to these arrangements of forms as *syntax*. The term "syntax" is most commonly used in relation to spoken or written language, but its root, which in Latin is *syntaxis*, means "to arrange."[19] Syntax is an arrangement of parts within a whole. In the arts, for example, a variety of terms relate to the problem of putting or arranging elements into a coherent structure. In music, composers and arrangers work with auditory elements; in the visual arts, painters determine the composition of visual elements; in architecture, architects arrange spaces. There are similar arrangements in dance, as well as in prose and poetry. Thus the term syntax need not be limited to discourse, whether spoken or written. It can, and originally did, refer to the more general problem of arranging elements within a whole.

If we examine the basis upon which elements are related within various forms of representation, it becomes clear that a continuum can be formulated on which it is possible to place individual forms of representation. At one end of the continuum are those forms of representation whose elements must be arranged according to a publicly codified set of rules. To use the elements within a form of representation skillfully, one must know the rules related to that form and how to use them. Consider simple arithmetic as an example. A specific rule or convention must be followed without deviation if arithmetic problems are to be dealt with correctly. A great deal of attention, particularly during early schooling, is devoted to helping children learn how to follow the rules in order to compute correctly. Similar rules hold for grammar, spelling, and punctuation. Although there is more leeway in the use of these forms for personal judgment, they are by nature largely *rule governed*. Learning to speak and write grammatically, like learning to spell and compute correctly, means, in part, learning how to follow codified rules. Indeed, it is precisely because the rules are codified and public that the skills related to their correct use are, compared to tasks where no comparable rules exist, relatively easy to teach and to evaluate. And this is why it is possible to say of a child's performance, when the child employs a form using a rule-governed syntax, that the answers are correct or incorrect. Such conclusions are impossible to draw in appraising the child's performance related to poetry, dance, music, or visual art.

At the other end of the continuum are those forms of representation that use a syntax that is more *figurative* than rule governed. The forms of representation about which I speak are exemplified, but not exhausted, by the fine arts, free verse, and literature. What the arts make possible—indeed, what they tend to elicit from those who use them—is an invitation to invent novel ways to combine elements. One of the reasons why form changes so rapidly in the arts, as compared to arithmetic, spelling, grammar, and punctuation, is because a premium is placed on productive novelty in the arts, ingenuity is considered a virtue. In spelling, it is considered a vice.

In saying, as I have, that the arts are not highly rule governed, I do not mean to imply that artistic conventions and social expectations do not influence what artists create. An artist wishing to produce a surrealist or op art painting fully understands that certain forms invented in the past will need to be reproduced by the artist in the present. A composer wishing to create a romantic symphony will feel a need to adhere to the formal structure of music created by romantic composers of the nineteenth century. In a sense, the "rules" are embedded in previous work. Anyone who wishes to produce similar work must observe those "rules."

But such "rules," if that is what they should be called, are not formally codified as they are for arithmetic, spelling, and punctuation. They are nowhere near as prescriptive in character, and they do not lead, as they do in spelling and arithmetic, to uniform solutions to common tasks or problems. A group of children given the same problem in arithmetic will, if they know the operations required, produce the same responses that, without ambiguity, can be judged correct or incorrect. Children asked to create a surrealist painting or a romantic melody will not be expected to and cannot in fact create identical solutions. The less rule-governed and more figurative the syntax, the more it permits idiosyncratic interpretation and novelty in form. Or, to put it another way, the further one moves away from conventional prescription, the more scope one has for personal choice. Thus, it is not surprising that the arts should be commonly regarded as providing optimal opportunity for personal expression, for cultivating, creativity and for encouraging individuality. What has been recognized intuitively is that the arts are forms that are not restricted to highly formalized rules. There is no such thing as an "incorrect" poem.

The distinction that I have made between syntaxes that are rule governed and those that are figurative might appear to be wrongheaded. After all, is not every painter or composer guided by rules that, when followed, lead to the creation of a form reflective of some artistic style, be it baroque, cubist, surrealist, or some other? And are not such styles the result of following the rules? A painter who wants to create an early cubist painting must obey the rules of early cubism: a restricted range of colors will probably be used, the surface features of an object will be broken into planes, the sides and back of an object will be seen as well as the front, and so forth. Is not learning how to paint or to compose or to write in a particular style the result of learning rules that are, in a sense, embodied within the style itself? If this is the case, then why differentiate between the rule governed and the figurative, even by degree?

There are several reasons for the distinction. In the first place, no painting or musical composition, no dance or poem is governed by rules wherein each element and combination among them is so specified that, by applying the rules to the performance or object made, one can without ambiguity determine if the performance or object is correct or incorrect. Although a sonnet by convention must have fourteen lines, no more and no less, what is artistically significant about a sonnet is not its fourteen lines but what it conveys. No rules can be applied for making this determination. Likewise, while an early cubist painter will use a restrictive range of colors and will break up forms into a series of planes, what makes the painting a work of art is not the fact that it follows those rules but that it generates a certain quality of experience in those who look at it in a competent way. For that achievement, there are no rules.

A second consideration is that, in rule-governed syntaxes, literal paraphrase is possible. One can translate the content of one form or statement into another without loss of meaning. The statement 85 plus 35 equals 120 means exactly what 35 plus 85 means, or 100 plus 20, or any other sum that equals 120. Because the rules of transformation are explicit, we can move from one formulation to another without losing information. There is no comparable translatability in forms of representation that emphasize figurative syntaxes. The form as a whole embodies its meaning. The relationships among its "parts" are unique configurations, and, when change is made in a "part," the meaning conveyed through the whole also changes. Furthermore, no codified set of rules can be applied in order to recover such meaning. Meaning depends upon judgment. The use of critical intelligence is a necessity. In short, one might say that syntaxes that are rule governed are codes; those that are figurative are metaphors. The rules for decoding codes are specific and public; for explaining metaphors, imagination is required.

Syntaxes at each end of the continuum, from rule-governed to figurative have different virtues. Rule-governed syntaxes increase the possibility of consensus or, in statistical terms, interjudge agreement. By specifying the rules to be applied to the elements within a form of representation, it is possible for anyone who knows the rules and their application to determine with a high degree of accuracy whether or not the operations have been performed correctly. In areas of human performance where personal choice or idiosyncratic interpretation or behavior is a liability—working on an assembly line, for example—it is extremely useful to work with forms of representation having a syntax whose use does not require imagination or even depend upon human judgment. In such situations, what one seeks is the correct application of a standard.[20] It becomes increasingly possible, as one uses forms of representation whose syntaxes are located at the rule-governed end of the continuum, to speak of correct or incorrect solutions or answers. As one moves toward the figurative end of the continuum, the terms "correct" and "incorrect" become increasingly inappropriate. What one might say about such solutions is that some are better or worse than others. It is here that deliberation and judgment become crucial, and it is in syntaxes operating at this end of the continuum that complex higher mental processes come into play.[21] The security of knowing when one is right or wrong is sacrificed for the uncertainty and fallibility that human judgment necessarily yields.

It is important to note that the almost exclusive emphasis in the elementary school curricula is on mastering forms of representation that emphasize rule-governed syntaxes. There may be several reasons for this. Probably the most important is that mastery of cultural conventions such as reading, writing, and arithmetic have an enormously important instrumental value. Without the ability to perform the operations these forms require, a student is severely handicapped as he or she advances in school. But it is perhaps even more important that the child's ability to deal with messages from the culture at large is severely impeded. It is clear that skill in the use of written and verbal language exceeds simple forms of rote learning. Interpretation is always to some degree necessary. Yet, at the elementary level, the emphasis is largely on learning the rules, knowing the correct ways to punctuate, to spell, to form letters, and to employ grammar. The rules of basic arithmetic operations are to be learned until they become rote; the less one has to think about how they are to be used, the better. Speed in the completion of arithmetic problems is one index of mastery since the more one has to think, the less one has mastered the rules.

Within the context of schools, mastery of the three Rs is a necessary condition for dealing with many other subjects the child will encounter, virtually all of which emphasize rule-governed syntaxes and place a premium on conventional modes of treatment. As they are typically taught, science, social studies, and geography tend to lean toward the rule-governed end of the continuum and employ conventionalized terms that the student must learn.

This prescriptiveness in curriculum, particularly at the early grades, may be emphasized for still other reasons. Because the rules of writing, reading, and arithmetic are public and codified, the tasks of teaching and evaluating student performance are made easier. In the typical math curriculum the teacher knows what problems are to be assigned, knows the specific operations the child needs to know in order to do these problems, and knows what counts as a correct solution. There is, compared to the teaching of literature, music, or art, little ambiguity about content, method, or conclusion. The textbook defines each; indeed, materials are available that allow students as well as teachers to "look up" the correct answer to each of the problems encountered.

One might well ask about the concomitant learning that goes on at school when the emphasis in curriculum is on forms of representation that emphasize rule-governed syntaxes and conventional modes of treatment. It seems quite likely that one of the things that children learn from a curriculum of this kind is that for every problem there is a correct solution. Furthermore, the teacher not only knows the solution, but knows what methods are to be used to achieve it. The child's problem becomes largely one of learning how to follow rules and to complete assignments —in short, to learn how to do what is expected by others who know what the correct answers are to problems encountered in school.

Now there is an appropriate sense in which teachers do know—indeed, they ought to know—what the answers are to the problems they set for students. I am not suggesting that there be cognitive parity between child and teacher. I am speaking of emphasis, of tone, of the pervasive quality of classroom life, and, most of all, of the need to understand what we neglect cultivating in classrooms—what I have called the "null curriculum."[22] Being educationally rigorous does not necessarily require going back several decades to dredge up mindless methods of teaching, rote forms of student performance, and docile obedience to the will of authority. Going back to the so-called basics is not good enough. Cognition is wider than the forms of representation that are common to propositional discourse and simple forms of arithmetic. To apply such solutions to the problems of improving the quality of education is to underestimate seriously the intellectual capacities children possess. How can such intellectual capacities be tapped? How can educational evaluation capture what is educationally significant about classroom life? It is toward a wider view of curriculum and evaluation that we turn next.

Notes

1. The notion "competent eye" refers to the fact that perception is both cognitive and transactional. Seeing is an achievement dependent upon visual literacy.

2. Images may be regarded as the generic process of creating mental structures through which the world is comprehended in science as well as in the arts.

3. No single form of representation can reveal all that can be experienced; hence, expression, like perception, is selective.

4. Habituation to particular forms of representation tends to increase both the skills and satisfactions secured from using them.

5. David R. Olson, "The Arts and Education: Three Cognitive Functions of Symbols," paper presented at the Terman Memorial Conference, Stanford University, October 26–28, 1978.

6. I am indebted to Rudolf Arnheim for this observation.

7. R. G. Collingwood, *The Principles of Art*, New York: Oxford University Press, 1958.

8. Aristotle writes "... as Agathon says, 'Art loves chance and chance

loves art.' Art, then, as has been said, is a state concerned with making, involving a true course of reasoning, and a lack of art on the contrary is a state concerned with making, involving a false course of reasoning; both are concerned with the variable." Aristotle, *Ethics*, ed., J. L. Ackrill, London: Faber and Faber, 1973, p. 116.

9. Harold Rosenberg, *American Painting Today*, New York: Horizon Press, 1965, p. 25.

10. Howard Gardner, *The Arts and Human Development*, New York: Wiley, 1973, pp. 29, 232.

11. Michael Cole, *Culture and Thought: A Psychological Introduction*, New York: Wiley, 1974.

12. Basil Bernstein, "On the Classification and Framing of Educational Knowledge," in *Knowledge and Control*, ed. M. Young, London: Collier, Macmillan, 1971.

13. Rudolf Arnheim, *Art and Visual Perception*, Berkeley: University of California Press, 1954. See esp. chap. 4.

14. R. L. Gregory, *Eye and Brain*, New York: McGraw-Hill, 1966.

15. Nelson Goodman, *Languages of Art*, Indianapolis: Bobbs-Merrill, 1968, p. 5.

16. E. H. Gombrich, "Visual Discovery through Art," in *Psychology and the Visual Arts*, ed. James Hogg, Middlesex, Eng.: Penguin Books, 1969, pp. 215–238.

17. See, for example, Arno A. Bellack, *Language of the Classroom*, New York: Teachers College Press, 1966; Ned A. Flanders, *Analyzing Teaching Behavior*, Reading, Mass.: Addison-Wesley, 1970.

18. Exemplification is used not only in teaching children, but also in the making of science. Model making is the effort to exemplify relationships.

19. Syntax derives from the Greek *syntaxis*, that is, "a putting together, a putting together of words, syntax." See Ernest Klein, *A Comprehensive Etymological Dictionary of the English Language*, New York: Elsevier, 1967.

20. John Dewey, *Art as Experience*, New York: Minton Balch and Company, 1934, See esp. Chap. 13.

21. Aristotle distinguishes between the deliberative, which is rationality applied to the variable, and the calculative, which is applied to the invariable and is "one part of the faculty which grasps a rational

principle." Deliberation is associated with practical wisdom, or "correctness of thinking . . . (while) searching for something and calculating. Aristotle, *Ethics*, ed. Ackrill, pp. 114, 122.

22. Elliot W. Eisner, *The Educational Imagination, on the Design and Evaluation of Educational programs*, New York: Macmillan, 1979.

4

Some Implications for Curriculum and Evaluation

The previous chapters examined some of the ways through which humans come to know the world and how they represent what they know to others. The dominating conceptions of cognition, intelligence, human achievement, evaluation, and research have been shaped by the belief that discourse and number are the central modes through which such operations are performed. To counter this view, I have argued that words and numbers, to be meaningful, depend upon concepts that are sensory in nature. I have argued, further, that words and numbers are only two forms through which representation takes place. I have provided this argument because I believe that the assumptions that we hold about the mind influence the practices and policies that shape our educational lives and that practices and policies that are based upon a limited view of cognition tend to lead to a limited conception of educational practice. The utility of my remarks about cognition and about what I have called "forms of representation" can only be determined by the kinds of changes in educational practice that this view suggests, whether or not immediate implementation is possible. I shall now identify the kinds of changes in school curriculum and in educational evaluation that can he implied from what I have had to say.

Change for the Curriculum

The implications for reform in curriculum that flow from the conception of mind and representation that followed my observations in Chapter 1 require an attitude toward schooling, mind, and education far more generous than is currently prevalent. In that sense, the orientation to education that I now describe is "out of phase" with the direction in which the nation has been moving. Yet to search for ways to devote more attention to what one believes is already overemphasized is not a particularly promising way to improve the quality of education. I do not believe giving students a larger dose of the three Rs is, in the long term, in the best interest of students. While any thinking individual wants children to read better, write better, and compute better (putting aside the seductively simple question of what "better" means), such aims, on balance, are not necessarily achieved by spending more time on what virtually everyone believes is not being done very well in the first place.

It is my belief that sound curriculum change will require a broader view of mind than is now salient in discussions of human ability. It also will require a willingness to free oneself from traditional views of the content of the curriculum and the methods of teaching. Old solutions, if indeed they ever were solutions, appear reassuring because they are known quantities, but reassurance and effectiveness are not identical. The prescriptions that emanate from the halls of ivy for more instruction in foreign languages, in science, and in math, the so-called hard subjects, might in some sense be educationally defensible. These prescriptions are, however, simplistic because they are unaccompanied by any semblance of theory or rationale. Such prescriptions are regarded as educationally virtuous because hard subjects are somehow believed to be good for students. It reminds me of the old educational bromide that "it doesn't really matter what students study in school as long as they don't like it." It is ironic that the same university professors who place such a high premium on theory and rational justification in their own fields feel so free to prescribe atheoretical and arational educational remedies for the public schools.

In this chapter I am not going to suggest that we wipe the educational slate clean and start all over. It is not necessary to discard the subjects that are now taught in the schools, for educational improvement is incremental.[1] What we need to guide incremental change is a forceful idea, an attractive conception, an image of man and the conditions that foster his development. And then we need a small place to begin. In this incremental process, an experimental attitude is critically important. In a certain sense what we desire to do we do not yet know how to do. The effort will be halting, it will require a willingness to take risks, we will make mistakes, it will require evaluation and revision at every step along the way. In contrast to those who have discovered the one right path, those who choose to swim against the tide must learn how to swim while they are doing it.

What, more specifically, would a school curriculum look like that embodied the conception of mind and representation that I described in the preceding chapters? In the first place, such a curriculum would be rooted in the idea that the pursuit of meaning is a major inclination of human beings, that meaning is something that humans construe rather than discover, that meanings are represented through a diverse array of forms, that each form that represents meaning provides it uniquely, and that educational programs should be designed so that "literacy" within these forms is achieved.

This would mean, first, that the scope of curriculum content would be expanded rather than diminished, and, second, that the manner in which the subject areas are now taught would be modified so that content within each subject area could be presented to and represented by the child in different ways.

Consider, first, the scope of the curriculum. If one accepts the views developed here, the almost exclusive curricular emphasis on discursive and numerical forms of representation would be modified in at least two ways. First, where discourse was employed, a far larger amount of it would be devoted to expressive and mimetic modes of treatment than is now the case. This means that the poetic, literary, and metaphorical—what I have called the expressive—uses of discourse would command much more attention than they now receive. The discourse used in schooling overwhelmingly employs conventional modes of treatment, and the numerical approach uses only the conventional modes. If we assume schools are interested in widening the child's access to meaning and accept the fact that different modes of treatment make different kinds of meaning possible and that competence in interpreting and using those modes is not an automatic consequence of maturation, then the school curriculum would be designed to develop such competencies. Incidentally, the major metalesson that children now learn when the mode of treatment is conventional and the syntax is rule governed is that there is a correct and an incorrect way of treating problems in schools.[2] There is little scope for idiosyncratic treatment or for judgment. The correct answers in the back of the book are regarded as the final authority. It is odd that, in a rationale for education that espouses the need for teaching children survival skills, the curriculum emphasizes forms of representation having a syntactical structure in which black-and-white, true-false, and correct and incorrect answers are dominant. The problems that most people have in their lives, the dilemmas that plague them most, are quite unlike the clear and unambiguous solutions found in school textbooks and workbooks. How do we prepare children for life by posing problems to them in which ambiguity is absent and the need for judgment rare?

Treating discourse in expressive and mimetic ways is one way in which the scope of the curriculum can be broadened. Another way is to give students access to subject areas that cultivate and refine the sensibilities. The subject areas that do this best are the fine arts. The fine arts —visual arts, music, dance, drama—were developed because of our human need to receive and convey information in forms that capitalize on the use of different sensory systems. Simply from the standpoint of mental health, the shift from one sensory system to another alters our consciousness. This in itself is important. Human beings become saturated, bored, and eventually withdraw psychologically if the opportunity to alter their state of mind is unavailable. If it is only from this standpoint, then, diversity in forms of representation in the curriculum should be considered a virtue. But it is by no means the prime virtue. The prime virtue is that the apotheoses of human achievement have been couched in such forms. If children are to have access to them, the curriculum must provide that access, and teaching must be geared so that the literacy required to construe meaning from them is possible. In the current educational climate, even the small amount of attention the fine arts once received in school programs is being eroded. In "good" educational times the average elementary school teacher devotes only 4 or 5 percent of the school week to the fine arts. Today the percentage is even less. As I indicated earlier, the same educational ideology that urges a return to the basics also sees the fine arts as being of peripheral importance in education. If the arts come to be regarded as nonintellectual or as essentially emotive in character, they will be considered merely a kind of diversion from the hard subjects having only the potential for cultivating avocational interests.[3] The realization that the arts represent one of the ways through which humans construct and convey meaning and that the creation of art forms requires the use of judgment, perceptivity, ingenuity, and purpose—in a word, intelligence—seems to have escaped most of those who have commented upon the state of education, not the least of whom are university professors sitting on admission committees and shaping admission policies for universities. A limited conception of intellect is not, however, the monopoly of professors who sit on admission committees. The faulty distinction between the cognitive and the affective has caused much mischief in both education and psychology. The idea that so-called affective subjects are noncognitive reflects the same bias held by those who believe that the arts are nonintellectual.[4]

I said earlier that the development of literacy in the various forms of representation requires that the curriculum be redesigned in two ways. Widening the array of forms of representation children encounter in school is the first such way. The second is the use of different forms of representation in the study of particular subject areas.

Assume for a moment that children at the junior high school level are studying family life in an effort to help them understand the roles that different family members play in the life of the family. We would like to help them grasp the idea that there are similarities and differences among these roles for families living in different cultures, and we want to help them become aware of the ways in which members of a family influence and are influenced by other people and institutions within the community. One way in which such an understanding can be secured is through social studies literature that uses a sociological frame of reference or explanation. But such an approach would be limited to what an author was able to put into discourse. If the discourse were mainly propositional, as it would be if sociological theory and data were employed, the discourse would be limited even further. There would be relatively little scope for the literary or poetic use of language. The meanings that children would be able to secure about family life would be constrained by the forms of representation used and the fact that the mode of treatment in this case would be conventional.

If, however, the study of the family included the use of literary resources—Oliver Twist, for example—or films of families from different cultures, or still photographs, or the poetry of Walt Whitman, and if, further, children were encouraged to express what they had learned about family life by using forms of representation that were not limited to propositions, a variety of ideas about such life might emerge that simply could not be expressed by some children through conventional prose.

The psychological ramifications of such an approach to problems and topics are significant. The data sociologists secure about the family, or the factory, or about group processes are not basically linguistic. The concepts of role, or social class, or status, or social structure do not wear name tags in the phenomenal world. They were initially imaginative perceptions of qualitative relationships that eventually were given a name. The terms used in sociological theory are shorthand devices that refer to empirical or imaginable qualities. Once formulated, they serve as guides to perception, but, before they can function in this way, the qualitative relationships to which they refer must be recognized. The point here is that, as children have access to and acquire competence in dealing with the information embedded within different forms of representation, they become, within that form, increasingly differentiated. As such differentiation occurs, the net with which they fish—to use Karl

Popper's analogy[5]—is woven even more finely; they pick up more and more information. Information developed out of highly differentiated perceptual systems can then be used as content for a form of representation, often in a form other than that in which the information was initially acquired. For example, consider the writer of literature. To be able to write, the writer must have something to write about. To have something to write about, the writer must be able to "read" the environment in which he lives. He must become aware of qualities of gesture and nuances of voices, he must have subtlety of vision. He must feel in his bones the places he writes about. Listen, as James Joyce writes:

> She leaned for a moment on his arm in getting out of the cab and while standing at the curbstone, bidding the others goodnight. She leaned lightly on his arm, as lightly as when she had danced with him a few hours before. He had felt proud and happy then, happy that she was his, proud of her grace and wifely carriage. But now, after the kindling again of so many memories, the first touch of her body, musical and strange and perfumed, sent through him a keen pang of lust. Under cover of her silence he pressed her arm closely to his side; and, as they stood at the hotel door, he felt that they had escaped from their lives and duties, escaped from home and friends and run away together with wild and radiant hearts to a new adventure.
>
> An old man was dozing in a great hooded chair in the hall. He lit a candle in the office and went before them to the stairs. They followed him in silence, their feet falling in soft thuds on the thickly carpeted stairs. She mounted the stairs behind the porter, her head bowed in the ascent, her frail shoulders curved as with a burden, her skirt tightly about her. He could have flung his arms about her hips and held her still, for his arms were trembling with desire to seize her and only the stress of his nails against the palms of his hands held the wild impulse of his body in check. The porter halted on the stairs to settle his guttering candle. They halted, too, on the steps below him. In the silence Gabriel could hear the falling of the molten wax into the tray and the thumping of his own heart against his ribs.[6]

To write such a passage Joyce had to experience, either directly or imaginatively, the lightness of a woman's arm against a man's body, the subtle comportment that constitutes a "wifely carriage," the musical, perfumed, and strange quality of a woman's body and of a man's desire. Such qualities are not words; they are experiences. James Joyce's genius resides in the twofold accomplishment of being aware of such qualities and being able to transform them through words so that the reader can envision the experience vicariously. The writer starts with vision but ends with words. He transforms the experience undergone into a verbal portrait. He renders a scene. The reader begins with Joyce's words but ends with vision. The words give rise to the experience that their referents make possible.

It would be a mistake to think that it is only the images that the individual words stimulate that account for our experience with the passage. The form of language also reveals. The expressive treatment of literary narrative conveys because of the tempo and the melody of how, as well as what, is said. For those who are unable to see, or to hear, or to taste, or to smell, the content of literature will be little more than something other people enjoy. School programs that neglect developing the child's literacy in forms of representation that sharpen the senses ultimately deprive the student of the very content he needs to use well the skills of reading and writing.

An awareness of the contributions of different forms of representation to human understanding is not something that one acquires simply by getting older. Indeed, in Western culture the opposite is more likely to be true. The term "understanding" is typically restricted to propositions about the world—something that can be looked up in a book or that can be verified through experiment. To expand this limited conception I suggest that an intentional and focused effort be made to help students become aware of how forms of representation shape the content conveyed. This, in a sense, is a request for a practical approach to epistemology.

One of the ways in which such understanding can be fostered is by designing curriculum activities that invite students to convey their understanding of, or reaction to, particular situations through the use of different forms of representation treated in the three modes. If we return to our example of the family, children could put together an exhibition that described what they believe to be the important aspects of life in the family, an exhibition that would convey what they had learned through photos, slides, and accompanying music and dialogue on cassette tape. They might portray what they had learned through poetry, or through story, or through dance, and, of course, through propositional discourse and number. Discussions could be held with children about what each form uniquely contributed, about the different kinds of information each contains, and about where and how they overlap. They could identify the problems associated with the creation of each, with the kinds of thinking and problem solving in which they engaged, and with the fullness of view that each, in combination, makes possible.

Such tasks are not simple. Outcomes are difficult to specify in advance. The attitude that must prevail is an experimental one. The teacher must be willing to work with children in small groups, as individuals, and collectively, as a class. Such pedagogical moves are not wholly consistent with the current trend toward highly prescriptive routines aimed at the achievement of known goals in forms that are propositional and that, perhaps most of all, can be measured. Yet the kind of educational practice I have described and even more the kinds of educational attitudes that it suggests seem to me to be of the utmost importance in any intellectually rooted conception of education. The preoccupation with prediction and control, two concerns of the utmost importance in running an assembly line, are not the most appropriate models for running a school.

The two types of curriculum practice I have described are intended to help students construe and appreciate the meanings embodied within different forms of representation. They are designed to increase students' ability to perceive qualities by inviting them to compare and contrast the kinds of meanings that different forms addressed to the same phenomena make possible. Such practices are, of course, closely related to Gestalt ideas about perceptual development. We start with wholes, perceiving at first the general and most obvious qualities or attributes of a form. Then, after perception has been funded, differentiation of perception occurs so that more subtle aspects, qualities, or attributes of the phenomena can be experienced. The use of contrasting examples for purposes of study and comparison is an effective way to foster such differentiation. Hence, one general curriculum practice that would characterize programs aimed at developing literacy in the various forms of representation would be to include a variety of forms so that access was possible, and another would be to invite children to study the different ways in which humans have represented what they have learned or imagined.

If such an approach to curriculum planning were implemented, other benefits would accrue. Because the use of a particular form of representation affects the ways in which phenomena are attended to and because each form of representation utilizes different mental skills, two consequences, both of educational value, are likely to occur. First, the angle from which a set of conditions was studied would expand. If one knew phenomena were to be represented visually, one would attend to the situation in a way that differed from the way in which one might attend to it if propositional forms of representation were to be used. If a student knew, say, that he would be expected to use at least two forms to represent what he had learned, it is likely that at least two angles of refraction would be employed.

Second, the kind of problem solving required to transform concepts into public forms depends upon both the nature of the concept and the character of the form to be used. Thus, for time to be represented, the use of number and the use of visual or auditory images present two very different kinds of intellectual demands. How does one represent time through number, through sound, through vision? By coping with such demands and then discussing the kinds of problems encountered, students develop skills and mental processes that can make an important contribution to their ability to read the messages that different forms of representation make possible.

Much is heard in discussions of education about the need to individualize instruction. Individualization is regarded as a prime pedagogical virtue, one that is based upon the recognition that children differ in their aptitudes, their interests, their prior experience, and their values, and that school programs and teaching methods should take these differences into account as educational decisions are made. When one examines individualized programs in American schools, one finds that the major variable that is altered for students is time; fast- and slow-learning students are given variable amounts of time to proceed through the same sequence of curriculum activities toward the same performance objectives. Such an approach to individualization alters only one of several variables that could have been changed. One could alter the goals of educational programs to suit differences in student interests and aptitudes, one could alter the content of instruction, one could alter the means through which the content was taught, one could alter the form through which students are expected to demonstrate what they learn. Individualization, in a subtle way, is related to the ideal of educational equity. Children having different aptitudes need to have an array of educational conditions that optimize their learning in school. If school programs provide only a very limited range of conditions, if they disregard certain forms of otherwise valuable human performance, if they restrict scholastic rewards to children who display only verbal or mathematical skills, they provide educationally inequitable opportunities to those students whose aptitudes and interests differ from the forms that are salient. Put another way, if the only game in town is chess and there are some very good poker players around, the poker players are culturally handicapped.

The idea that educational programs ought to be designed to help each child realize his or her unique learning potential has been articulated by a host of writers, but perhaps no one has put the case more incisively than the great English philosopher, poet, and art critic, Sir Herbert Read, when he identified what he believed to be the two major principles on which education could rest.[7] One, he said, was to help children become what they are not; the other was to help them become what they are. The former was standard practice in totalitarian societies where children were shaped into an image defined by the state. The latter principle was one that he believed was the basis of social harmony and rich cultural life. Education was to provide the conditions that would help potential become actualized. Aptitudes for the visual or the mathematical, for the propositional or for the auditory, should be cultivated so that self-realization was possible. Such conditions in the school would do much to mitigate the frustrations of stifled talents which Read believed led to social conflict. In addition, the realization of such potential would contribute significantly to the creation of a graceful and culturally rich society because of the actualized talents that each member had to contribute. Read is not alone in this view. Speaking of the physical costs of unfulfilled potential, the American poet John Ciardi, addressing a group of powerful, practical-minded businessmen, had this to say:

> There is no poetry for the practical man. There is poetry for the man-kind of the man who spends a certain amount of his life turning the mechanical wheel. For if he spends too much of his time at the mechanics of practicality he must become something less than a man or be eaten up by the frustrations stored in his irrational personality.
>
> An ulcer, gentlemen, is an unkissed imagination taking its revenge for having been jilted. It is an unwritten poem, an undanced dance, an unpainted watercolor. It is a declaration from the mankind of the man that a clear spring of joy has not been tapped and that it must break through muddily, on its own.[8]

Herbert Read and John Ciardi present essentially the same views, but convey them in a form of representation treated in different modes.

What does the issue of individualization and educational equity have to do with the thesis I have developed in this book? Equity of educational opportunity cannot be provided if some children are not given the chance to use and develop their most potent intellectual abilities. By diversifying the forms of representation that are made available in school and by according them a status equal to the status now accorded the three Rs, we might be able to expand the success that some children achieve in school to those who now find schools places in which only particular, limited varieties of human ability count. Students who are told both formally and informally, implicitly and explicitly, covertly and overtly that their particular interests and aptitudes are unimportant, that they are nonintellectual, that they will not be taken into account when the students are seeking admission to a university are being denied equal educational opportunity. That is the current situation in American education, and the press for a return to the basics will exacerbate rather than ameliorate that trend.

In arguing the case for curriculum diversification in a manner related to the ways in which humans conceptualize and represent those conceptions to themselves and others, I am not suggesting that attention to the skills of reading, writing, and computing be abandoned. These skills are of central importance as techniques for handling information. I am arguing that attention to other forms of representation is also needed and that, at present, the range is being constricted rather than expanded. I argue, furthermore, that, by broadening our conception of literacy and developing those literacies through especially designed curricula, the skills of reading, writing, and computing will themselves improve. Reading, for example, requires an ability to hear the melody of a paragraph, to visualize the scene as portrayed, to feel the pulse and power of a trenchant passage. To write requires the ability to see, to hear, and to feel the world so that the writer will have a content to express and a desire to share it with others. Such achievements are not educationally marginal. Attention to the development of multiple forms of literacy should not be regarded as a diversion from what is important in schools; rather, it is at the very heart of what education requires.

Change for Educational Evaluation

And what of educational evaluation? There are two areas in educational evaluation where, in my view, changes need to be made. The first is conceptual; the second is practical.

Perhaps the primary conceptual change upon which practical change depends (although this is not to suggest that conceptual change must necessarily precede practical change; the latter can and often does bring about the former) is the way in which meaning and knowledge are conceptualized. As I have already indicated, at present both concepts are restricted largely to propositions about empirical matters and to the use of scientific or scientific-like procedures for validating the claims such propositions make. What needs to be recognized within the educator's professional culture is something that I believe is already recognized in the educator's personal life, namely, that propositions have no monopoly on meaning, that meaning is conveyed through a variety of forms, and that each form is itself nonredundant in the kind of meaning that it provides. Extending this recognition to professional matters is, I believe, of fundamental importance in the epistemology of educational inquiry. As long as nonpropositional forms of representation are regarded as untrustworthy, as subjective projections, as psychological reports that have more to say about their creator than about the world they describe, propositions will continue to be regarded as the only dependable avenue to understanding.

What I am suggesting here, I suppose, is something like, but not quite, a paradigm shift among those in the educational community. I say "not quite" because I am not advocating the replacement of one paradigm for another. It is not a matter of replacing a Newtonian universe with an Einsteinian one; rather, it is a willingness to recognize the essential incompleteness of any single form of representation and, hence, the desire to conceptualize and describe the world through several forms.

I do not want to give the impression that no progress has been made toward this end. The work that the Northwest Regional Educational Laboratory has done in enabling educators from various parts of the country to develop their ideas about the ways in which meanings are conveyed in film, folklore, and music, for example, is itself noteworthy.[9] And if the annual meetings of the American Educational Research Association are any indication, the incidence of papers devoted to epistemological issues and to the development of new models of evaluation has increased dramatically. These indicators suggest that, among those in higher education, an awareness of the limits of conventional assumptions and methods and the desire to exceed the boundaries these assumptions and methods necessitate have been developing. Indeed, even among those who were trained to use a strictly psychometric paradigm there are some who have either shifted their focus altogether or have provided support for those who never were psychometrically oriented. Yet as promising as these developments are, they apply to a very small percentage of those in the educational research and evaluation communities. Mainstream practices are still of a conventional variety, and the sympathetic, indeed receptive, attitude among some toward nonconventional approaches to evaluation is still regarded with suspicion or as a passing romantic phase by many more. And as for the public schools, the press of the back-to-basics movement with its demand for more standardized evaluation has created a climate that is inhospitable to approaches to evaluation that do not provide quantitative results. It is almost as though the aspiration to grade students as eggs and milk are graded is considered a desirable goal for schools in the United States.

What must happen, whether before or after the means for producing nonconventional forms of evaluation emerge, is that educators must recognize that to restrict the use of forms through which man represents what he knows means that a restricted form of understanding will result. The corollary is that, by using a variety of forms of representation, forms of understanding can be developed that would not otherwise be possible. Such awareness is far from widespread in higher education.

The development of such awareness will not by itself be enough to make practical differences in the way in which we conduct our educational lives. If new approaches to evaluation are to be employed, at least two conditions need to be established. First, the new forms of representation that are employed need to be used with high levels of skill. Second, those to whom the message is directed need to be able to read it. Put another way, both encoding and decoding skills must be present if the effort is to be useful.

The achievement of such skills has particular implications for institutions of higher learning, both in the training of teachers and in the training of educational evaluators. Programs need to be developed that will help prospective evaluators learn how to use media that are now all but absent from such programs. Consider film as an example. The use of film as a means through which to represent and evaluate educational situations requires skills that are both artistic and technical: artistic in the demands made upon the filmmaker to put a coherent and revealing picture together; technical in the demands made to handle equipment competently and to process the materials employed. The artistic use of film production as an evaluative tool requires also that one understand the possibilities of film for employing the *modes* of representation I described earlier. For some purposes, mimetic rather than expressive modes may be more appropriate. For other purposes, the opposite may be the case. The point, however, is that anyone attempting to portray a complex situation can benefit from the options he or she knows and can use.

Training programs for the use of film in evaluation would have a theoretical as well as a technical dimension. Indeed, the theoretical aspect of evaluation and training far exceeds training that is directly relevant to filmmaking per se. What one chooses to photograph is influenced by what one believes to be educationally significant. Significance in educational matters is never simply a technical issue. It is a matter of valuing and seeing value in the situations of schooling. How one applies educational theory in order to interpret the concrete circumstances of educational life, whether in classrooms or on celluloid, should be a major point of focus in such training.

When mention is made of the use of film or music or literary narrative as a part of the technical repertoire that should be available within university departments of education to those prospective evaluators who seek such training, the absence of such opportunities becomes vividly apparent. Few professors on the faculties of schools of education have such skills themselves. Not all—indeed, not even most—universities have departments of cinematography in which such skills can be acquired. And even where they do, links between the school of education and the department of cinematography need to be forged. Such relationships often involve political problems of one kind or another. I do not mention these obstacles to dissuade people from moving in this direction—quite the contrary. Without an understanding of the present situation and the obstacles that have to be overcome, the prospects for successful program building are dim.

What I have said about the need to develop skills in filmmaking exemplifies the need in other areas as well. If literary prose is to be used as a prime vehicle for representing what one has learned about a school, a classroom, a teacher, or a pupil, the skills of narrative writing and reading need to be developed. These are not particularly well developed in graduate schools of education. As a matter of fact, in some institutions students are actively discouraged from writing expressively. Expressive writing is considered soft, impressionistic, nonrigorous, unscientific, romantic, nonprofessional, unscholarly, and nonintellectual. To write in a scholarly, professional way, particularly when writing research reports, students are encouraged to be "objective," which means that nonexpressive language is to be used and that third person singular or the first person plural forms are to be employed. The use of "I" is regarded as too personal and, hence, subjective.

Although such expectations might be regarded by some as relatively unimportant forms of professional socialization—on their surface they do not appear to be significant—such expectations symbolize an entire universe of values, a universe that has excluded until quite recently what might be regarded as humanistic forms of representation in professional writing. The relatively recent willingness among some scholars and some institutions to make room for the use of artistic paradigms is encouraging. Professors who operate in that mode themselves are needed on faculties of education, both to provide models that students can emulate and because such people possess skills that can be taught to students who wish to work in this mode. Approaches to evaluation that exploit the expressive power of language also require people who are capable of reading what has been written and know how to evaluate its merits. One of the most difficult problems students who use this mode of writing have is to find professors who do *not* want to apply social science criteria to evaluate it.[10] As the number of such faculty increase, students will have an easier search, and the political climate of schools of education will become, I hope, more tolerant and less parochial.

The point regarding the ability of an audience to read and appropriately appraise evaluation studies written in an expressive mode is of crucial importance. As long as such modes of treatment are regarded as untrustworthy, the probability of their use in education is small. As long as they are absent in our efforts to understand the processes and effects of educational practice, to that extent will our understanding of those processes and their consequences be limited, even biased.

How shall the profession prepare itself to produce such evaluations skillfully? How shall those who work in the public schools and who support those schools be enabled to read the messages that such evaluations embody? In addition to collaboration among departments within the university and the creation of training programs with schools of education, relationships between school districts and schools of education need to be developed to provide settings where evaluation programs using such forms can be undertaken, where the problems of doing such evaluation can be confronted, where different groups having different responsibilities and different needs can come together to discuss and appraise the utility of what has been done, and where university professors and their students can learn from their mistakes and their achievements.

What I am suggesting is the creation of partnerships between school districts and schools of education, partnerships that provide the conditions for work to be conceptualized and tested among people responsible for the conduct of educational practice. At present, most of what is tested in educational research, and to a lesser degree in educational evaluation, is tested by the peers of those who produce it: university professors. I suggest that such an audience is too narrow. Evaluation efforts jointly conceived and undertaken provide a more realistic forum for appraisal and debate and, through it, a better chance to improve the process of both educational research and educational evaluation.

What such new relationships may mean for staffing patterns within school districts, I cannot say for certain. They do suggest that districts will need to identify individuals on their staffs to serve as liaisons with university departments and schools of education, preferably people who can speak both the language of the school district and the language of the university. If some sort of parity between the two is to occur, both parties will need to contribute their share.

Because publication in professional journals and participation in professional meetings is so significant in the upward mobility of university professors, changes in format and use of equipment will also need to be made for the presentation of work that is in a nondiscursive form of representation. What this means is that the paper-reading format that is ubiquitous at professional meetings will need to be modified so that presentations on film or videotape or through drama are possible. It means also that professional journals will need to make place for visuals that are now largely absent. By the use of visuals in journals, I do not mean simply using pictures to make journals more attractive but, rather, using visuals in relation to written analyses that are designed to reveal the qualities of educational life that only pictures can reveal and that, without them, might otherwise go unseen. In this regard, the use of visuals in Roland Barthes's work in semiotics is exemplary:[11] visuals and verbal analysis interact to provide the reader with an understanding of images that could not otherwise be achieved. It is this dialogue between theory and nonverbal forms of representation that is so potentially illuminating for educational evaluation. There is a great deal to be learned about classrooms and schools from seeing what they look like.

To use such means as vehicles for conveying what has been learned through evaluation will require, as I have suggested, a set of conditions that encourages scholars to use nondiscursive forms of representation in their published and presented work. At present, the use of such materials, and the equipment that is necessary, is a problem at most conventions, just as it is for those journal editors whose image of scholarship consists of a particular version of the printed word. When these gates, the gates of convention presentation and professional journals open more widely, the incentives for such work will also increase. And when the incidence of reports that make use of nondiscursive forms of representation increase, the conception of what research and evaluation mean will also broaden. In short, access to program time and to the pages of professional publications will not only give those who choose to employ nonconventional means of evaluation and research the opportunity to do so, but it will, by its growing presence, restructure our conception of what counts as educational research and evaluation.

Another conceptual issue that needs attention deals with the need to recognize the different functions that evaluation performs in education and the appropriateness of different forms of representation for improving these functions. If, for example, one is attempting to determine achievement on criterion-referenced tasks, say being able to swim ten lengths of a pool in order to be permitted to go on a canoe trip through a white water rapid, the most unambiguous form of representation to employ is number. One wants to count the number of lengths a person can swim. If, however, one wants to know about the way in which the criterion was or was not met, then one needs a description of the process. For this, a visual and a discursive form of representation would be more appropriate.

The point here is that the choice of what form of representation to emphasize in evaluation depends, or should depend, upon the purposes to be served. Given the fact that evaluation efforts are used to achieve different purposes, there is no reason to believe that one form of representation will be appropriate for all of them.

But the problem of deciding what form of representation to employ in educational evaluation goes beyond the question of the intended function of the evaluation. Even in the example given above of selecting individuals who can swim well enough to take a canoe trip on white water, the educational aims for the individuals involved are complex rather than simple in character. We are not only interested in teaching children to swim and enjoy canoe trips, but we also want them to feel good about themselves, we want to help them to learn how to learn, we want them to hold values that will lead to personal satisfaction and are socially constructive. In short, even when we have clear-cut educational goals such as teaching children to swim, in education we are always interested in more than what the goal or goals of the course specify. Hence, evaluation procedures, if they are to be instrumental in the achievement of complex educational goals, need to be useful for determining more than whether simple goals were achieved. Knowing that certain gains in reading were achieved, for example, tells us little about the quality of education if we know nothing about the processes that led to those gains. Some gains might not be worth the price paid for their achievement. In terms of evaluation practices, this suggests that a wider, more diversified net is likely to provide a more balanced view of what the processes entailed. With such a view, a more intelligent appraisal can be made of the results achieved.

Perhaps one more example might drive the point home. Many secondary schools are now making available to students courses specifically designed to help them increase their scores on the Scholastic Aptitude Test. In addition, private schools operated for profit are also offering such courses. Let us assume that such courses are effective and that, as a result of a twenty-week course of study, students' scores on the SATs increase by ten points on the verbal and ten points on the mathematical sections of the test. If we evaluate the effects of such programs only in terms of the scores obtained, we neglect a host of other considerations that could have substantial educational ramifications. For example, what has the student given up in order to take such a course? What does a school-sponsored course aimed exclusively at raising test scores say to students about the values of the educational process? What kinds of pedagogical methods are employed and what do these methods teach the student in addition to answers to the questions they find on the SATs? How would one secure data to answer the questions just posed? What role would visuals perform? What might be done with tape-recorded materials, with expressive narratives? What might interviews with students and teachers reveal? In other words, if one wanted a full picture of the educational costs and benefits of an educational policy or practice, what kinds of data would one seek and in what forms would it be represented?

I have suggested that a restricted use of the forms through which what is known is represented of necessity limits what one can convey. Quantification and propositional discourse, as precise as they might be, as useful as they are for obtaining high levels of consensus, can never tell the whole story. The extent to which we are restricted by convention or by competence to their use alone is the extent to which we will secure a limited view of the processes and consequences of educational practice.

The use of forms of representation in educational evaluation need not occur independently; they can be used in combination to highlight or vivify what one wishes to convey. Film and drama are excellent vehicles for such use. Recently I saw a television program that dramatically illustrated the effectiveness of combining forms of representation. The particular program made use of clips from the film, *One Flew over the Cuckoo's Nest*, interspersed with clips from a film showing the mental hospital in Salem, Oregon, where *One Flew over the Cuckoo's Nest* was filmed. Clips from the Hollywood version showed patients lining up to receive their daily medication, and they were juxtaposed with scenes of actual patients receiving such medication. Medication was distributed in the form of pills to be swallowed with water in small paper cups. The medication was distributed to patients four times a day.

The difference between the two versions was that, in the Hollywood version, a kind of ballet music accompanied the shots of patients slowly walking in line to be medicated. What the music did, particularly because of its balletic character, was to provide a contrapuntal element in the scene in order to highlight the fact that the hospital staff had found a relatively simple way to keep patients in a placid and compliant state of mind by administering tranquilizing medication of one kind or another. The music combined with the visuals called the viewers' attention to the contribution the hospital was making to the patients' stuporous way of life. Without the impact of the music, the significance of what was happening might have been missed.

But let us suppose that some of the patients really needed the medication. Let us suppose that at least some of this medication was essential to their physical and psychological well-being. If so, then is not such a portrayal misleading? Does it not bias the viewer negatively? Is it not a caricature of what the hospital is trying to accomplish?

The answers to such questions may well be positive. Nevertheless, by highlighting the way in which the hospital staff administered the drugs, almost through a seemingly mindless routine, the question of its mindlessness can be raised, and the use of the drugs can be explained, the manner in which the pills were provided can be discussed, the need for patients to ingest drugs on a regular basis can be examined. As Clifford Geertz commented regarding the contributions of ethnography, "it raises," he said, "the level of discourse through which we vex each other."[12] Portrayals, through the combination of forms of representation, also have the potential to raise the level through which we vex each other, not necessarily by providing "The Truth," but by bringing to our critical consciousness practices about which we had been only dimly aware.

Consider another example of how the combination of forms of representation can convey meanings not possible by using them one at a time. Figure 2 is a reproduction from an advertisement that appeared in a British newspaper.[13] What we find here is a brilliant use of a propositional form of representation combined with a visual one. The gradually increasing use of space between sentences, words, and letters slows the pace of the reading, thus reinforcing the message expressed in the prose. The gradual use of increased space is something the reader does not notice until the end of the narrative. Like the elderly poor who, without heat or proper diet, succumb to the winter's cold and gradually die, the reader, too, finds himself unaware that his pace is slowing, and he eventually comes to the end of the article by hanging onto an uncompleted word. Completion is prematurely terminated.

Through imaginative and sensitive combination of forms of representation such as these, people are helped to achieve levels of consciousness that might otherwise have fallen by the wayside. Because such forms are neither prosaic nor humdrum, the reader cannot simply provide a stock response. A new level of consciousness is achieved because a new form of mutually supporting forms of representation have been welded together to make an important point.

Can the use of such forms be productively employed in educational evaluation? I believe they can. Might the use of such forms convert educational evaluation into a new form of fiction, something that manipulates the reader's or the viewer's attention and interpretation of educationally relevant phenomena? Might not educational evaluation take on the trappings of Hollywood productions and Madison Avenue advertis-

When you're old you can become cold without even noticing it. Often without so much as a shiver.

You simply slow down.

Soon you can't be bothered to make yourself a proper meal. A slice of toast will do. And why build up the fire? You feel all right. You don't notice your body getting colder.

And you slow down.

The next thing you don't notice is your mind slowing down. Did you order the coal? You can't remember. Never mind.

Now you've really slowed down.

You feel drowsy. Even the effort of going to bed seems too much. You just nod off in the chair.

It doesn't seem to

matter any mor

Figure 2. Use of a Combined Propositional and Visual Form of Representation.

ing? Might we not through such techniques lose our status as objective professionals and dispassionate scholars seeking essentially the creation of understanding through the discovery of truth?

Such concerns rest at base on the belief that there is a royal road to understanding and that a particular set of methods, especially as they approximate the methods employed in the natural sciences, are the means to that end. Concerns such as these also rest upon the belief that such methods are relatively free from preconception or bias or loaded language. What is not understood, it seems to me, is that the very categories that one employs, permeated as they are with images, shape the perception of events, influence the way in which those events are interpreted, and define the terms through which what has been learned can be conveyed to others. There is no such thing as a "pure" conception or a value-free form of expression. All dimensions of phenomena that can be attended to do not receive equal time. To exploit the power of human conception, to tap and employ its versatility in the interest of disclosure, deliberation, and understanding, seems to me to be a virtue we should seek. Our own critical capacities are not to be set aside in the analysis of materials such as I have described. Such materials can, in fact, provide the content for critical analysis. I am not, therefore, urging a shift in allegiance from one paradigm to another; I am urging the exploration and exploitation of the potential of other paradigms and other forms of representation to illuminate the qualities and values of educational life.

Notes

1. For a brilliant analysis of the practical and incremental character of curricular change, see Joseph Schwab, "The Practical: A Language for Curriculum," *School Review*, 78: 1–23, November 1969.

2. "Metalessons" are a part of the implicit curriculum. See Elliot W. Eisner, *The Educational Imagination: On the Design and Evaluation of Educational Programs*, New York: Macmillan. 1979, esp. chap. 5.

3. Elliot W. Eisner, "The Role of the Arts in the Invention of Man," *New York University Quarterly*, 11:2–7, Spring 1980.

4. This view that the arts are affective and, hence, inferior to mathematics and the sciences has its roots in Plato's theory of knowledge. See Books 6 and 7 of *The Republic*, tr. and introd by Francis MacDonald Cornford, New York: Oxford University Press, 1951.

5. Karl Popper, *The Logic of Scientific Discovery*, London: Hutchinson, 1959.

6. James Joyce, *The Dead*, in *Six Great Modern Short Novels*, New York: Dell, 1946, pp. 47–48.

7. Herbert Read, *Education through Art*, New York: Pantheon Books, 1943. See esp. chaps. 1 and 2.

8. John Ciardi, "An Ulcer Gentleman is an Unwritten Poem," *Canadian Business*, 1954.

9. The Northwest Regional Educational Laboratory has supported the work of numerous scholars interested in exploring new approaches to educational evaluation. The papers that have been prepared are available from that laboratory.

10. It is understandable that professors who have been professionally socialized into the use of social science criteria should want to apply it to nonscientific approaches to evaluation. It is one of the ways in which individuals handle cognitive dissonance.

11. Roland Barthes, *Mythologies*, New York: Hill and Wang, 1978.

12. Clifford Geertz, *The Interpretation of Culture*, New York: Basic Books, 1973.

13. Health Education Council, "Winter Warmth, Sudbury, Suffolk, England," in *The Guardian*, January 24, 1980, p. 5.

Index